ROBERT J. MARZANO

JULIA A. SIMMS

Questioning Sequences in the Classroom

MARZANO
—Research—

THE **CLASSROOM** STRATEGIES **SERIES**

555 North Morton Street
Bloomington, IN 47404
888.849.0851
FAX: 866.801.1447

email: info@marzanoresearch.com
marzanoresearch.com

Visit **marzanoresearch.com/classroomstrategies** to download the reproducibles from this book.

Printed in the United States of America

Library of Congress Control Number: 2013955921

ISBN: 978-0-9858902-6-1 (paperback)

18 17 16 15   3 4 5

Editorial Director: Lesley Bolton

Managing Production Editor: Caroline Weiss

Production Editor: Tara Perkins

Text and Cover Designer: Amy Shock

Compositor: Laura Kagemann

MARZANO RESEARCH DEVELOPMENT TEAM

Director of Publications

Julia A. Simms

Production Editor

Katie Rogers

Marzano Research Associates

Tina Boogren

Bev Clemens

Jane Doty Fischer

Jeff Flygare

Maria C. Foseid

Mark P. Foseid

Tammy Heflebower

Mitzi Hoback

Jan K. Hoegh

Russell Jenson

Jessica Kanold-McIntyre

Sharon V. Kramer

David Livingston

Pam Livingston

Sonny Magaña

Beatrice McGarvey

Margaret McInteer

Diane E. Paynter

Debra J. Pickering

Kristin Poage

Salle Quackenboss

Laurie Robinson

Ainsley B. Rose

Tom Roy

Gerry Varty

Phil Warrick

Kenneth C. Williams

Visit **marzanoresearch.com/classroomstrategies**
to download reproducibles from this book.

CONTENTS

Italicized entries indicate reproducible forms.

CHAPTER 3

EXTERNAL SOURCES OF INFORMATION 33

CHAPTER 4

RESPONSE STRATEGIES 59

CHAPTER 5

PREPARATION FOR QUESTIONING SEQUENCES 75

ABOUT THE AUTHORS

Robert J. Marzano, PhD, is the cofounder and CEO of Marzano Research in Denver, Colorado. During his forty years in the field of education, he has worked with educators as a speaker and trainer and has authored more than thirty books and 150 articles on topics such as instruction, assessment, writing and implementing standards, cognition, effective leadership, and school intervention. His books include *The Art and Science of Teaching*, *Leaders of Learning*, *On Excellence in Teaching*, *Effective Supervision*, *The Classroom Strategies Series*, *Using Common Core Standards to Enhance Classroom Instruction and Assessment*, *Vocabulary for the Common Core*, and *Teacher Evaluation That Makes a Difference*. His practical translations of the most current research and theory into classroom strategies are known internationally and are widely practiced by both teachers and administrators. He received a bachelor's degree from Iona College in New York, a master's degree from Seattle University, and a doctorate from the University of Washington.

Julia A. Simms, EdM, MA, is director of publications for Marzano Research in Denver, Colorado. She has worked in K–12 education as a classroom teacher, gifted education specialist, teacher leader, and coach, and her books include *Coaching Classroom Instruction*, *Using Common Core Standards to Enhance Classroom Instruction and Assessment*, and *Vocabulary for the Common Core*. She has led school- and district-level professional development on a variety of topics, including literacy instruction and intervention, classroom and school-wide differentiation, and instructional technology. She received her bachelor's degree from Wheaton College in Wheaton, Illinois, and her master's degrees in educational administration and K–12 literacy from Colorado State University and the University of Northern Colorado, respectively.

ABOUT MARZANO RESEARCH

Marzano Research is a joint venture between Solution Tree and Dr. Robert J. Marzano. Marzano Research combines Dr. Marzano's forty years of educational research with continuous action research in all major areas of schooling in order to provide effective and accessible instructional strategies, leadership strategies, and classroom assessment strategies that are always at the forefront of best practice. By providing such an all-inclusive research-into-practice resource center, Marzano Research provides teachers and principals with the tools they need to effect profound and immediate improvement in student achievement.

INTRODUCTION

Questioning Sequences in the Classroom is part of a series of books collectively referred to as *The Classroom Strategies Series*. This series aims to provide teachers, as well as building and district administrators, with an in-depth treatment of research-based instructional strategies that can be used in the classroom to enhance student achievement. Many of the strategies addressed in this series have been covered in other works, such as *Classroom Instruction That Works* (Marzano, Pickering, & Pollock, 2001), *Classroom Management That Works* (Marzano, 2003), *The Art and Science of Teaching* (Marzano, 2007), and *Effective Supervision* (Marzano, Frontier, & Livingston, 2011). Although those works devoted a chapter or a part of a chapter to particular strategies, *The Classroom Strategies Series* devotes an entire book to an instructional strategy or set of related strategies.

We begin with a brief but inclusive chapter that reviews the research and theory on questioning. Although you may be eager to move right into those chapters that provide recommendations for practice in schools, we strongly encourage you to examine the research and theory, as it is the foundation for the entire book. Indeed, a basic purpose of *Questioning Sequences in the Classroom* and others in *The Classroom Strategies Series* is to present the most useful strategies based on the strongest research and theory available.

Because research and theory can provide only a general direction for classroom practice, *Questioning Sequences in the Classroom* goes one step further to translate that research into applications for questioning in schools. Specifically, this book suggests a unique strategy for classroom questioning: questioning sequences. Research indicates that the intentional use of targeted questions in a coordinated sequence is an effective way to elicit students' prior knowledge, prompt the discovery of new information, and deepen and extend students' learning in all content areas.

Chapter 1 reviews history, research, and theory relevant to classroom questioning practices. One of the major conclusions of the chapter is that individual questions do not promote deep understanding and higher cognition as effectively as questioning sequences. In this book, we present questioning sequences in four phases: the detail phase, the category phase, the elaboration phase, and the evidence phase. In chapter 2, we describe and exemplify each phase and give teachers concrete and specific guidance about how to immediately implement questioning sequences in their classrooms. Chapter 3 explains how to teach students to glean information from all types of texts to answer questions during each of the four phases of a questioning sequence. To answer questions, students will need to use information from one of two potential sources: prior knowledge or external sources. These external sources might be traditional print texts, graphic texts, multimedia texts, electronic texts, Internet texts, or others.

Chapter 4 highlights different response techniques that teachers can use when students are responding individually or working in groups to answer questions. We also review a number of techniques that teachers can use to facilitate group interaction as students work collaboratively. Finally, chapter 5 gives teachers detailed guidance about how to plan questioning sequences that occur during a single class period or stretch across several classes.

Throughout the book, we exemplify various strategies using classroom vignettes. These narratives describe how each strategy might look in a teacher's classroom. This allows readers to see how our suggestions apply to their grade level and content area(s). Additionally, appendix B (page 97) presents examples of questioning sequences for each grade level K–12. These focus on a variety of content areas, including reading, writing, mathematics, and science.

How to Use This Book

Educators can use *Questioning Sequences in the Classroom* as a self-study text that provides an in-depth understanding of effective questioning in the classroom. As you progress through the chapters, you will encounter comprehension questions. It is important to complete these questions and compare your answers with those in appendix A (page 89). Such interaction provides a review of the content and allows a thorough examination of your understanding. Groups or teams of teachers and administrators who wish to examine the topic of questioning in depth may also use *Questioning Sequences in the Classroom*. When this is the case, teams should answer the questions independently and then compare their answers in small- or large-group settings.

Chapter 1

RESEARCH AND THEORY

Despite its popularity as an instructional strategy, classroom questioning has been the subject of educational debate in the United States for more than one hundred years. To the surprise of many, the extant research does not clearly describe the exact nature of effective questioning.

The debate regarding questioning began in 1912, when Romiett Stevens investigated teachers' questioning practices. One of the variables she examined was how many questions teachers ask each day. She reported that "the average number of questions for a day's activity is 395" (p. 15) with questions consuming "eight-tenths of the school time" (p. 6). Since Stevens's work, various researchers have examined the frequency of classroom questions and reported similar results (see table 1.1). Obviously, the sheer volume of questions asked each day renders questioning an important variable in the classroom.

Table 1.1: Research Findings Regarding Number of Questions Asked by Teachers

Floyd, 1960*	On average, primary teachers asked 348 questions each during a school day.
Moyer, 1966*	On average, elementary school teachers asked 180 questions each during a science lesson.
Schreiber, 1967*	On average, fifth-grade teachers asked 64 questions each during a thirty-minute social studies lesson.
Dunkin & Biddle, 1974	Compiled research (Dahllöf & Lundgren, 1970; Furst, 1967; Furst & Amidon, 1967) indicated that one-tenth to one-sixth of all classroom interactions occur in the form of questions asked by the teacher.
Nash & Shiman, 1974	Despite teachers' perceptions that they asked 12–20 questions each half hour, they actually asked 45–150 questions each half hour.
Levin, 1981	Compiled research (Floyd, 1960; Gall, 1970; Schreiber, 1967; Stevens, 1912) indicated that teachers asked 300–400 questions in a typical school day.
Gambrell, 1983	Third-grade teachers asked a question every 43 seconds.

*As cited in Gall, 1970.

Probably the most important finding from Stevens's (1912) research was that in some classes, asking many questions improved student performance, but in other classes, it did not. Simply asking questions, then, might not be an advisable classroom practice. This finding should have spawned immediate concern about how best to ask effective questions. Unfortunately, it wasn't until decades later that the nature of effective versus ineffective questions was systematically addressed.

Early Conceptions of Effective Questioning

Beginning in the 1950s, researchers started studying effective questioning in earnest, operating under the principle that, once identified, effective questioning techniques could be explicitly taught to teachers, thus improving student performance. This effort required researchers to develop "sophisticated methods of systematic observation and analysis" (Wilen & Clegg, 1986, p. 153). Specifically, they needed a way to classify questions. Meredith "Mark" Gall (1970) identified a number of question classification systems that were created between 1950 and 1970 (including Adams, 1964; Aschner, 1961; Carner, 1963; Clements, 1964; Gallagher, 1965; Guszak, 1967; Moyer, 1966; Pate & Bremer, 1967; Sanders, 1966; and Schreiber, 1967). In many of these systems, researchers classified questions using existing models of types of cognition. For example, Mary Jane Aschner (1961) based her question classification system on Joy Paul Guilford's (1959) "Three Faces of Intellect" model. The most well-known of these efforts was Norris Sanders's (1966) adaptation of Bloom's (1956) taxonomy to questioning types.

Although its original purpose has been mostly forgotten, Bloom's taxonomy was initially written to help university examiners (people who write tests for university students) design assessment items. Benjamin Bloom (1956) and his colleagues sought to develop a reliable system for classifying skills and knowledge into educational objectives. This purpose was explicit in the book's title, *Taxonomy of Educational Objectives: The Classification of Educational Goals*. Bloom's taxonomy classified educational objectives into six hierarchical levels: knowledge (1.00), comprehension (2.00), application (3.00), analysis (4.00), synthesis (5.00), and evaluation (6.00). As Lorin Anderson and his colleagues explained in their 2001 revision of Bloom's taxonomy,

> With the Taxonomy in place, examiners do not have to approach every objective as a unique entity. Rather, they can say to themselves, "Oh, this is an analysis objective. I know how to write examination items for analysis objectives." They can pull out their "templates" . . . and, with modifications dictated by differences in subject matters, write several items in a fairly short time. (p. 35)

In other words, the taxonomy was designed to make the task of writing assessment items for various educational objectives (or learning goals) easier. In their original publication, Bloom (1956) and his colleagues were careful to warn against overextension of the taxonomy:

> It should be noted that we are not attempting to classify the instructional methods used by teachers, the ways in which teachers relate themselves to students, or the different kinds of instructional materials they use. We are not attempting to classify the particular subject matter or content. What we are classifying is the *intended behavior* of students—the ways in which individuals are to act, think, or feel as the result of participating in some unit of instruction. (p. 12)

When they revised Bloom's taxonomy in 2001, Anderson and his colleagues extended this caution, saying, "specifying a learning objective does not automatically lead to a prescribed method of instruction" (p. 257). Bloom, Anderson, and their colleagues were very careful to note that the levels of the taxonomy were *never designed* to classify instructional methods such as questioning, or how teachers relate to students, as in a classroom discussion.

Bloom's Taxonomy: A Misapplied Framework

Although Bloom's taxonomy was well intended and quite useful when applied to its original purpose (classifying educational objectives), it soon became the default framework for questioning hierarchies, thanks in large part to Norris Sanders. In 1966, he published the book *Classroom Questions: What Kinds?* There, he proposed that Bloom's taxonomy should be used to classify questions and defended his decision by saying,

> Some teachers intuitively ask questions of high quality, but far too many overemphasize those that require students only to remember, and practically no teachers make full use of all worthwhile kinds of questions. The objective of this book is to describe a practical plan to insure [*sic*] a varied intellectual atmosphere in a classroom. The approach is through a systematic consideration of questions that require students to *use* ideas, rather than simply to *remember* them. (p. 2)

Sanders (1966) acknowledged that applying Bloom's taxonomy to questions was not its intended purpose, stating that "some explanation is necessary to show how a book on objectives [Bloom's taxonomy] has significance to the topic of questions" (p. 2). Although Sanders provided an explanation for his adaptation of Bloom's taxonomy, his rationale did not address the limitations of Bloom's taxonomy as a questioning framework in at least four ways.

First, Sanders assumed that because Bloom and his colleagues provided example test items for each level of their taxonomy, they were suggesting that their taxonomy was useful for classifying classroom questions. Referring to Bloom and his colleagues, Sanders (1966) stated,

> One of the ways they defined each category was by using examples of questions that required students to engage in the specified kind of thinking. . . . Bloom and his associates claim that any objective can be classified in their taxonomy and *imply* that any question can also be classified. (pp. 3, 7, italics added)

But Bloom (1956) and his colleagues explicitly warned against the assumption that classifying questions is the same as classifying objectives. In the preface to their example test items, they stated,

> The task of classifying test exercises [that is, questions] is somewhat more complicated than that of classifying educational objectives. Before the reader can classify a particular test exercise he must know, or at least make some assumptions about, the learning situations which have preceded the test. He must also actually attempt to solve the test problem and note the mental processes he utilizes. (p. 51)

As stated by its authors, using Bloom's taxonomy to classify test items (and, by inference, questions) is more complicated than using it to classify educational objectives. While it is possible to classify questions, using a taxonomy specifically designed for educational objectives to classify questions was an extrapolation not necessarily recommended by the taxonomy's authors. Classifying questions requires a system created specifically for that purpose.

Second, Sanders (1966) proposed no systematic method for classifying questions using Bloom's taxonomy, and his research revealed that teachers often disagreed about what level of the taxonomy a question represented:

> Experience shows that teachers working with the taxonomy of questions often disagree on the classification of a question and that all parties to the dispute can make good cases for their positions. (p. 7)

However, Sanders dismissed this issue, saying,

> This is not a severe handicap in the uses anticipated for the classroom teacher. . . . The important
> point for teachers to remember is that difficulty in classifying any question is no detraction from the
> quality of the question. (pp. 7–8)

Unfortunately, Sanders did not offer further direction as to how teachers should address their disagreements or resolve issues in classifying questions. This inability to definitively classify a question presented a serious limitation in the use of Bloom's taxonomy for questioning.

Third, Sanders (1966) claimed that his classification system would promote critical thinking. However, Sanders defined *critical thinking* as "all thought processes beyond the memory category. A teacher who offers his students appropriate experiences in translation, interpretation, application, analysis, synthesis, and evaluation can be assured he is providing instruction in every intellectual aspect of critical thinking" (p. 6). This definition reveals a limited understanding of the nature and function of critical thinking. In effect, Sanders equated all types of thinking beyond recognition and recall with higher levels of thought. Although this has some intuitive appeal, it is certainly an oversimplification of the construct of critical thinking and does not offer enough detail and guidance to teachers to produce the intended effect of complex questions—namely, that students think deeply and rigorously about content.

Fourth and finally, for Sanders's recommendations to be completely valid, the cognitive level of a question should correlate with the cognitive level of the answer it elicits. That is, if a teacher asks a higher-order question, he or she assumes that it will prompt a higher-order answer from a student. However, this is not always the case. If a student has already heard the answer to a higher-order question, he will not have to engage higher-order cognition to answer the question. He can simply recall the answer he heard previously. For example, a teacher might pose what she thinks is an evaluation prompt: Compare the advantages and disadvantages of solar power and decide whether it would be a good decision to install solar panels in your family's home. If a particular student's family had just installed solar panels in their home, and the student had been included in his parents' discussion of pros, cons, and the final decision, the student simply recalls the information he already knows. This situation does not necessarily require evaluative or higher-order thinking from the student. As seen here, asking a higher-order question does not guarantee that a student will use higher-order processes to answer it. Sanders (1966) seemed to equivocate on this issue. He initially stated, "A certain kind of question leads to a certain kind of thinking" (p. 8), but later noted that "it is wrong to assume that a question inevitably leads to a single category of thinking or that all students are necessarily using the same mental processes to arrive at an answer" (pp. 8–9). As shown here, Bloom's taxonomy was subject to certain limitations that restricted its effectiveness as a questioning framework.

The problems inherent in using Bloom's taxonomy, or any other taxonomy based on levels of cognitive processes, were not lost on researchers. In his 1970 article, "The Use of Questions in Teaching," Gall surveyed the literature on questioning since Stevens's work in 1912 and made recommendations for future research. In addition to reiterating the importance of questioning and the idea that teachers ask a lot of questions (see table 1.1, page 3), Gall highlighted the following weaknesses (similar to those outlined in this chapter) in using cognitive process models to classify questions:

> A weakness of the cognitive-process approach to question classification is that these processes
> are inferential constructs. Therefore, they cannot be observed directly. . . . It is not always possible
> to know whether a student answered a particular question by using a high-level cognitive process,
> such as analysis or synthesis, or by using the relatively low-level process of knowledge recall. (p. 710)

Gall's review also touched on the question that would consume research on questioning for the next two decades: Are higher-order questions better?

An Examination of Higher-Order Questions

Sanders's (1966) central premise was that certain types of questions were better or more desirable than others. As noted previously, he stated that "some teachers intuitively ask questions of high quality, but far too many overemphasize those that require students only to remember" (p. 2). This statement implies that questions that only require students to remember or recall information are of low quality.

Gall (1970) speculated that the stigma surrounding "fact" or "recall" questions (also referred to as memory questions, knowledge questions, lower-cognitive questions, or lower-order questions) was largely due to the well-established idea that teachers ask a great many of them. He explained,

> Educators generally agree that teachers should emphasize the development of students' skill in critical thinking rather than in learning and recalling facts. . . . Yet research spanning more than a half-century indicates that teachers' questions have emphasized facts. . . . It is reasonable to conclude that in a half-century there has been no essential change in the types of question which teachers emphasize in the classroom. About 60% of teachers' questions require students to recall facts; about 20% require students to think; and the remaining 20% are procedural. (pp. 712–713)

Gall gave several suggestions as to why teachers ask these questions, including the following:

- Fact questions are needed to bring out the information required to answer critical thinking questions.

- Critical thinking and problem solving have only recently been incorporated into curriculum materials, and teachers' questioning behaviors haven't caught up yet.

- The curriculum materials teachers use emphasize fact questions.

- Teacher training programs don't teach effective questioning skills.

Whatever the reasons for the widespread use of "fact" or "recall" questions, Gall reaffirmed the research supporting their prominence in the classroom.

Early Research on Questioning Levels

The beginning of the 1970s marked an important milestone in educational research. Studies relating specific teaching strategies to student achievement became popular; this type of research was known as process-product research (Dunkin & Biddle, 1974). Researchers examined various instructional strategies to see if there were links between specific teacher actions and student achievement. Regarding teachers' questioning behavior, researchers focused on the effects of asking questions at different cognitive levels. Very often, Bloom's taxonomy was used to designate "higher-order" and "lower-order" questions.

Early researchers reported widely differing results. Francis Hunkins (1968) found that higher-order questions increased student achievement, but the test that he used to measure student achievement was multiple choice, a question type not well suited to the measurement of higher-order thinking, which is more open ended and abstract. Gall (1970) characterized Hunkins's findings "as only suggestive" (p. 715), stating, "it seems a distortion . . . to put the question types into a multiple-choice format since some types, such as evaluation questions, do not really have a 'correct' answer" (p. 714). Five years later, and again using multiple-choice tests, Frank Ryan conducted two experiments (1973, 1974) to examine the cognitive levels of teachers' questions. In the first study (1973), he found that "high level questions are more efficient than low level questions for moving students toward low and high level understandings" (p. 66). But in the second study (1974), he found that lower-order questions could be just as effective in promoting higher-order understandings as higher-order questions. He observed,

> To conclude that achievement is merely a function of question-type (e.g., high, low), appears overly simplistic. . . . Research on questioning which is confined solely to considerations of the kinds of questions being posed, is too restrictive and potentially limited in terms of instructional inferences. (p. 74)

Michael Dunkin and Bruce Biddle echoed the same sentiment in their 1974 review of questioning research. They concluded that the types of questions teachers ask are not strongly related to student achievement but also highlighted the bias that would increasingly affect researchers and educators over the next fifty years: "While . . . it appears self-evident that teachers should place more stress upon such higher-level processes as *synthesis* and *evaluation*, no evidence has appeared to date suggesting that this stress will give desired product effects" (p. 243). In effect, researchers and educators found it difficult to believe that higher-order questions were not in some way superior to lower-order ones.

Barak Rosenshine (1976b) issued a call to re-examine the conventional wisdom about questioning. After explaining earlier research findings (Brophy & Evertson, 1974a; Gage & Stanford Program on Teaching Effectiveness, 1976; Soar, 1973; Stallings & Kaskowitz, 1975; Ward & Tikunoff, 1975), which showed that lower-order questions led to greater student achievement, he stated,

> The continual bromides that factual questions are bad and higher level questions are good were not supported by well-designed research. . . . The lack of significant results for complex or higher level questions has puzzled all the researchers, and led us to conclude that we need to rethink what is meant by types of questions and their effects. (pp. 61, 63)

In 1978, Gall and his colleagues reaffirmed the equivocal nature of questioning research; they examined and conducted research on the cognitive level of questions and found "no clear relationship between the frequency with which the teacher uses higher cognitive questions and student achievement. . . . Contrary to the belief held by many educators . . . emphasizing fact questions rather than higher cognitive questions is the more desirable teaching pattern" (pp. 177, 196). Like Rosenshine, they referred to their findings as "puzzling" (p. 196), further illustrating the entrenched assumption among educators that higher-order questions must somehow be better than lower-order questions. Other synthesis studies continued to find mixed results.

In 1979, Philip Winne reviewed eighteen studies regarding teacher questioning behavior and concluded that "whether teachers use predominantly higher cognitive questions or predominantly fact questions makes little difference in student achievement" (p. 43). He continued, "Few studies in the traditional body of research on teaching, and none of the experiments reviewed here, have documented that higher cognitive questions actually promote the assumed cognitive processes in students" (p. 44). In 1981, Tamar Levin expressed surprise that "lower order questions tend to be positively related to achievement, while high order classroom questions tend to be unrelated to achievement. These findings and conclusions contradict educators' and researchers' assumptions" (p. 29). As in previous studies, the finding that higher-order questions had little to no effect on student achievement created surprise and confusion among researchers and educators.

The Rise of Higher-Order Questions

In 1981, Doris Redfield and Elaine Rousseau diverged from the previous trend of conclusions. Using a technique called meta-analysis, they reanalyzed the data from Winne's 1979 study and calculated a rather large effect size for the use of higher-order questions (0.73). Effect sizes tell how powerful a classroom strategy is: the higher the effect size, the more effective the strategy. The average effect size for most education interventions is 0.40 (Hattie, 2009), so 0.73 represented a claim of significant effectiveness. Interestingly, although Redfield and Rousseau used the same data as Winne, their conclusions were the exact opposite of his. Nevertheless, researchers and educators rallied around Redfield and Rousseau's study, giving it greater weight and more prominence than previous synthesis studies. Researchers who had previously been cautious about questioning levels seemed to take Redfield and Rousseau's study as confirmation of the supremacy of higher-order questions.

In 1984, Gall again reviewed research on teachers' questioning behavior (including Dunkin & Biddle, 1974; Redfield & Rousseau, 1981; Rosenshine, 1976a; and Winne, 1979). Although three of the four studies in his review (all except Redfield and Rousseau) found either no effect or a negative effect for higher-order questions, Gall stated that "research indicates that an emphasis on higher cognitive questions would be more effective" (p. 42) and "researchers have found that emphasis on higher cognitive questions generally produces better learning than emphasis on fact questions" (p. 45). Gall's newfound enthusiasm for higher-order questions was shared by other researchers. Nathaniel Gage and David Berliner (1984) affirmed their positive beliefs about higher-order questions in the third edition of *Educational Psychology*. They used Redfield and Rousseau's synthesis as their primary source, stating,

> Asking higher-level questions "works" in the sense of making students behave at relatively higher levels of cognitive processing. Higher-order questions seem to make students go through higher-order mental processes—processes requiring kinds of reasoning other than mere recall. Such questions may be justified on that basis alone. (p. 636)

These researchers' enthusiasm notwithstanding, mixed findings about higher-order questions persisted.

The Continuation of Mixed Findings

It is important to note that there were some who remained cautious about the questioning research, despite Redfield and Rousseau's (1981) findings. In 1986, Jere Brophy and Thomas Good reviewed a wide body of research on teacher questioning (including Brophy, 1973; Brophy & Evertson, 1974a, 1974b, 1976; Clark et al., 1979; Dunkin, 1978; Evertson & Brophy, 1973, 1974; Gall et al., 1978; Redfield & Rousseau, 1981; Ryan, 1973, 1974; Soar, 1968, 1973, 1977; Soar & Soar, 1972, 1973, 1978, 1979; Stallings & Kaskowitz, 1974; Winne, 1979; and Wright & Nuthall, 1970). They cautioned,

> The data reviewed here on cognitive level of question, and even meta-analyses of these and other relevant data (Winne, 1979; Redfield & Rousseau, 1981) yield inconsistent results. *The data do refute the simplistic (but frequently assumed) notion that higher-level questions are categorically better than lower-level questions.* (p. 363, italics added)

In 1986, William Wilen and Ambrose Clegg said of higher-order questions, "Of all the questioning practices presented related to effective teaching research, this is the most tentative because of the conflicting findings" (p. 156).

Finally, in 1987, Gordon Samson, Bernadette Strykowski, Thomas Weinstein, and Herbert Walberg sought to resolve the tension between Winne's (1979) and Redfield and Rousseau's (1981) reviews. Samson and his colleagues reanalyzed the same studies used by Winne and Redfield and Rousseau and computed a far smaller effect size (0.13) for higher-order questions than Redfield and Rousseau (0.73). Samson and his colleagues stated,

> The present quantitative synthesis of studies on the effects of higher cognitive questioning suggests that it has a small effect on learning measures (median effect size = .13). . . . This synthesis contradicts Redfield and Rousseau's (1981) previous large and inexplicable estimate of questioning effects. It supports Winne's (1979) conclusion that large, consistent effects remain to be demonstrated. (p. 294)

In other words, Samson and his colleagues replicated Redfield and Rousseau's study and found different results. The results were so different, in fact, that Samson and his fellow authors claimed that their work actually supported Winne's 1979 conclusion that there is no relationship between higher-order questions and student achievement.

The Continuing Bias for Higher-Order Questions

By 1987, the issue of higher-order versus lower-order questions was "the most thoroughly investigated issue in questioning research" (Gall & Rhody, 1987, p. 31). At best, researchers looked at the compiled research with a skeptical eye. At worst, they advocated for higher-order questions and ignored research to the contrary. In response to the groundswell of support for higher-order questions, checklists began to appear that allowed principals or other observers to count how many higher- and lower-order questions a teacher asked during a lesson (Wilen, 1987). Lists of question stems for each level of Bloom's taxonomy became a staple of teacher training programs. Many authors and researchers advocated for higher-order questions, often without citing any research at all.

The knowledge base regarding questions did not change much with the advent of the new millennium. In their book *Learning to Question, Questioning to Learn*, Marylou Dantonio and Paul Beisenherz (2001) summarized the situation as follows:

> Many educators and researchers, even today, cling to the presumption that in order to improve student achievement and enhance learning, teachers must ask higher-level questions. . . . Years of studies on higher-level versus lower-level teacher questions and the effect of these questions on student achievement were at best confusing, and at worst disillusioning. . . . The debate between higher-level versus lower-level questioning to influence student achievement continues to the present day, with no clear answers. (pp. 26–27)

Throughout the 1990s and the first decade of the 2000s, educators seemed to accept the assertion that higher-order questions were better, that Bloom's taxonomy should be used to classify questions, and that the conflicting research results from the 1970s and 1980s should be mostly ignored.

Where We Are Today

What can the interested educator conclude from the research conducted since the publication of Sanders's influential book in 1966? The answer is best illustrated in table 1.2.

As can be surmised from table 1.2, the research on higher- versus lower-order questions is equivocal. There is no clear indication as to the superiority of one versus another. As Good and Brophy (2003) aptly observed,

> Research findings based on such classifications have been mixed and relatively uninformative about when and why different kinds of questions should be used. The research underscores the complexities involved and cautions against attempts to substitute simple formulas for careful planning of question sequences. (p. 378)

They went on, saying,

> It is not true that higher-order or complex questions are always better than lower-order or simpler questions. . . . Even to phrase the issue this way is to impose a false dichotomy. Varying combinations of lower-order and higher-order questions will be needed, depending on the goals that a teacher is pursuing. Guidelines need to focus on *sequences* of questions designed to help students develop connected understandings, not just on the cognitive levels of individual questions considered in isolation from one another. (p. 378)

Table 1.2: Studies Examining the Relationship of Question Levels to Student Achievement

Lower-Order Questions Are More Effective	No Difference or Inconclusive Results	Higher-Order Questions Are More Effective
Wright & Nuthall, 1970[a]	Spaulding, 1965[c]	Kleinman, 1965[a]
Soar, 1973[b]	Millett, 1968[a]	Hunkins, 1968
Stallings & Kaskowitz, 1975[b]	Rogers, 1968[a]	Ladd & Anderson, 1970[a]
Gage & Stanford Program on Teaching Effectiveness, 1976	Rosenshine, 1971[b]	Buggey, 1971[a]
Rosenshine, 1976b	Savage, 1972[a]	Aagard, 1973[a]
Gall et al., 1978	Martikean, 1973[a]	Beseda, 1973[a]
Clark et al., 1979[a]	Bedwell, 1974[a]	Ryan, 1973
Soar & Soar, 1979[b]	Brophy & Evertson, 1974a	Lucking, 1975[a]
	Dunkin & Biddle, 1974	Redfield & Rousseau, 1981
	Ryan, 1974	Gayle, Preiss, & Allen, 2006
	Gall, 1975[b]	
	Ghee, 1975[a]	
	Rosenshine, 1976a	
	Mathes, 1977[a]	
	Winne, 1979	
	Hare & Pulliam, 1980	
	Levin, 1981	
	Ripley, 1981[a]	
	Brown & Edmondson, 1984	
	Brophy & Good, 1986	
	Samson et al., 1987	

[a]As reported in Gayle et al., 2006.
[b]As reported in Rosenshine, 1976a, 1976b.
[c]As reported in Levin, 1981.

In this book, we take the position that past problems with classroom questioning stemmed from a misplaced focus on trying to classify individual questions. Ivan Hannel (2009) explained that "most teachers have been given snippets of information about questioning—including lists of question-stems to consider or recitations of Bloom's Taxonomy as a scaffold for questioning—but few teachers have been taught a practical pedagogy of questioning" (pp. 65–66). We propose that the current practice of using Bloom's taxonomy to classify individual questions is an ineffective scheme around which to frame teacher questioning. Instead, we assert that it is more effective for teachers to use series of questions that cultivate and deepen students' understanding of the content. We refer to these series of questions as *questioning sequences*.

Questioning Sequences

Recent research has begun to explore better questioning schemes that focus on questioning sequences as opposed to individual questions. In 2007, Harold Pashler and his colleagues summarized a body of recent research on questioning (including Beck, McKeown, Hamilton, & Kucan, 1997; Craig, Sullins, Witherspoon, & Gholson, 2006; Driscoll, Craig, Gholson, Ventura, & Graesser, 2003; Gholson & Craig, 2006; Graesser & McMahen, 1993; Graesser & Olde, 2003; King, 1992, 1994; Otero & Graesser, 2001; Rosenshine, Meister, & Chapman, 1996; and Wisher & Graesser, 2007) and made recommendations for teachers' classroom practices. Pashler and his colleagues acknowledged that "students typically need considerably more time to answer deep questions than they would to answer more superficial questions" (p. 30) but, refreshingly, neither vilified questions that ask students to recall knowledge nor glorified questions that ask students to think more deeply. Each has its place and plays an important role in student learning through questioning.

Questioning sequences lead students to create, elaborate on, and defend generalizations about facts and details related to the content. Dantonio and Beisenherz (2001) observed that

> consistently, the literature on effective questioning practices has insisted that questioning sequences are far more effective in promoting student understanding than any one type of question (Beyer, 1997; Costa & Lowery, 1989; Dantonio, 1990; Gall, 1970; Gall et al., 1978; Klinzing & Klinzing-Eurich, 1987; Riley, 1981; Wilen, 1991; Wright & Nuthall, 1970). (p. 37)

Good and Brophy (2003) further stated that "issues surrounding cognitive level of questions should take care of themselves if sequences of questions are planned to accomplish worthwhile goals that are integral parts of well-designed units of instruction" (p. 379). In other words, questioning sequences use specific types of questions in an intentional sequence to guide students through the thinking necessary to generate deep understanding of the content and its implications.

Translating Research and Theory Into Practice

In this text, we use the research and theory presented in this chapter and from books such as *The Art and Science of Teaching* (Marzano, 2007) to create a unique approach to questioning. We regard a questioning sequence as a series of questions or prompts that ask students to articulate details about the content, identify characteristics of content-related categories, generate elaborations about the content, and provide evidence and support for those elaborations. The questioning sequence concept presented here is specifically designed to guide students through the process of making a claim by collecting information, categorizing it, drawing a conclusion, and providing evidence to support it. The following chapters expand on this concept and give teachers concrete direction and guidance as to its use.

Chapter 2

QUESTIONING SEQUENCES

One generalization supported by the research described in chapter 1 is that accurately classifying a single question in terms of whether it elicits higher-order or lower-order cognition in students is difficult if not impossible. This is necessarily the case because a question will require lower-order cognition (such as recall) from a student if that student already knows the content, regardless of its complexity. For example, consider the following question: Why is it that tides are equally high on both sides of the earth when the moon's gravity is pulling from only one side? If a student has not been previously exposed to the answer to the question, he will need to engage in higher-order reasoning, such as the following:

> I know that the moon has gravity and that high tide occurs on opposite sides of the earth at the same time. When the moon's gravity pulls on the water in Earth's oceans, it probably causes high tide on the side of the earth closest to the moon. But what about the side of the earth that isn't facing the moon? Maybe the moon's gravity is also pulling on the earth's core, creating a counterforce pushing away from the earth on the other side. That would also explain spring and neap tides: when the sun, moon, and earth are in a straight line, the pull is stronger, creating greater tidal fluctuation, or spring tides; when the moon is at a right angle to the sun with the earth at the vertex, the pull is weaker, creating less tidal fluctuation, or neap tides.

Of course, this type of thinking on the part of the student would be considered higher order because it involves mentally manipulating the effects of multiple forces and drawing conclusions. However, if the student had heard or read this explanation and stored that information in long-term memory, the thinking elicited by the question would be simply recall.

In effect, any scheme to focus on one specific type of question (for example, "higher-order" questions) to the neglect of another type (for example, "lower-order" questions) is most probably doomed to failure. However, an approach that attempts to elicit deeper and more rigorous thinking in students by asking various types of questions in a specific linear sequence has great promise.

A Model for Questioning Sequences

We believe that an effective questioning sequence has the following four phases:

1. Questions about details

2. Questions about categories

3. Questions that require students to elaborate on their previous answers

4. Questions that require students to provide evidence for their elaborations

Unlike Bloom's taxonomy, which is often perceived as a hierarchy applied to individual questions (thus prioritizing some types of questions over others), the questioning sequence in figure 2.1 is designed as a series of four phases of questions with a common theme and goal. Each phase is as important as every other phase.

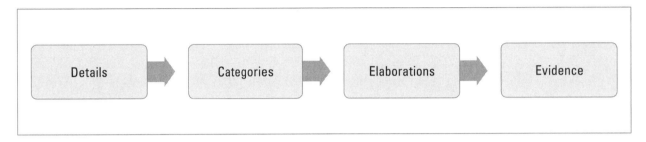

Figure 2.1: Elements of an effective questioning sequence.

Questioning sequences should be based on the established instructional goals for a unit, which are often derived from a set of standards. Chapter 5 (page 75) explains in detail how a teacher can analyze standard statements to identify specific knowledge and skills students are expected to learn, and base questioning sequences on those objectives. Appendix B (page 97) provides extensive examples of goals and questioning sequences derived from standards. As indicated in figure 2.1, questioning sequences usually start with details.

For example, an English language arts (ELA) teacher focusing on the goal of students using end punctuation appropriately, derived from the standard that students will "demonstrate command of the conventions of standard English capitalization, punctuation, and spelling when writing" (National Governors Association Center for Best Practices & Council of Chief State School Officers [NGA & CCSSO], 2010a, p. 25), might begin a questioning sequence by asking one or more detail questions about end punctuation:

- When is it appropriate to use a question mark?

- When is it appropriate to use a period?

- What type of end punctuation would you use in each of the following sentences?

  - I think we can go now

  - Doesn't anybody want to come with me

  - Look what I can do

  - I wonder how old he is

Next, the teacher asks questions about a category to which end punctuation belongs. In this case, a logical category is general punctuation. The teacher might ask students questions such as:

- What are some other types of punctuation that help us know when a sentence is over?

- How is a semicolon different from a period in terms of what it is telling the reader?

Once questions have been asked and answered about a category to which details belong, the teacher asks elaboration questions. These questions typically ask students to explore why. For example, the teacher might ask, "Why do you think we tend to see relatively few colons (compared to periods or question marks) used in writing?" Elaboration questions usually require students to go beyond what they were explicitly taught or what they already know. The final stage in a question sequence is to ask students to provide evidence for their elaborations. This is tantamount to asking students, How do you know your answer is accurate? For example, assume that a student answered the elaboration question about colons in the following way:

> I think people use fewer colons than periods or question marks because colons do the same thing as periods (they are used at the end of independent clauses) and because fewer people understand how to use them properly.

The teacher asks the student to provide some evidence for her statement. The student provides examples of independent clauses followed by periods or colons (pointing out that most independent clauses can easily end with periods and do not need colons), or the student finds a quote about the use of colons from a valid Internet source that supports her explanation. In the following sections, we consider each of the four phases of a questioning sequence in depth.

Phase 1: Detail Questions

Details are the building blocks of complex ideas and mental constructs. That is why it is highly unfortunate that detail questions have been belittled in past discussions of lower-order versus higher-order questions. In fact, questions about details should be designed to carefully and accurately draw out and develop students' knowledge base about specific topics. This is not necessarily an easy task because a given topic addressed in class can have many different details. As stated previously, the key to identifying what to focus on is to have a clearly stated learning goal or objective. In the following example, we explain how a social studies teacher focusing on the goal that students will understand "the major developments and chronology of the Revolutionary War and the roles of its political, military, and diplomatic leaders (e.g., George Washington, Benjamin Franklin, Thomas Jefferson, John Adams, Samuel Adams, John Hancock, Richard Henry Lee)" (Kendall & Marzano, 2000, p. 144) would design a questioning sequence to guide students as they learn about the role of the United States' political leaders during the American Revolution and their influence on subsequent political figures.

As he begins to design the questioning sequence, the social studies teacher discovers that there are many pertinent details related to the American Revolution about which he might ask questions, including:

- People associated with the American Revolution (for example, George Washington, Benjamin Franklin, Thomas Jefferson, Abigail Adams, Paul Revere)

- Organizations and groups associated with the American Revolution (for example, colonists, patriots, loyalists, the Founding Fathers, Native Americans, the French)

- Intellectual or artistic products associated with the American Revolution (for example, Declaration of Independence, U.S. Constitution, Bill of Rights, "Paul Revere's Ride" by Longfellow)

- Naturally occurring objects or animals associated with the American Revolution (for example, tea, horses, tobacco, cotton)

- Naturally occurring places associated with the American Revolution (for example, Boston Harbor, Appalachian Mountains, Atlantic Ocean)

- Manmade objects associated with the American Revolution (for example, printing press, rifle, flag)

- Manmade places associated with the American Revolution (for example, Boston, Lexington, Concord, Charleston, Saratoga, New York, Fort Ticonderoga)

- Events associated with the American Revolution (for example, Battle of Bunker Hill, Battles of Lexington and Concord, Battle of Yorktown, siege of Charleston, First Continental Congress, Second Continental Congress, Boston Tea Party, enactment of the Stamp Act)

- Natural phenomena associated with the American Revolution (for example, winter at Valley Forge, Great Hurricane of 1780)

- Physical actions associated with the American Revolution (for example, marching, firing a rifle, using a bayonet, riding a horse)

- Mental actions associated with the American Revolution (for example, drafting the Declaration of Independence, planning battle strategies)

- Feelings generated by or experienced during the American Revolution (for example, rebellion, fear, sorrow, joy)

- Human constructs associated with the American Revolution (for example, democracy, freedom, liberty, social contract, natural rights)

All of these types of details are legitimate topics for questioning. As previously mentioned, a teacher determines a focus for detail questions based on what he or she wishes to emphasize over the course of the entire questioning sequence. This emphasis is normally found in the learning goals or target outcomes for the unit. For example, if a learning goal stated that students would understand how various *people* influenced the American Revolution, the teacher could focus detail questions on specific people such as George Washington, Benjamin Franklin, Thomas Jefferson, Abigail Adams, Paul Revere, and so on. If the learning goal asked students to understand organizations and groups associated with the American Revolution, then the teacher could ask questions about colonists, patriots, loyalists, the Founding Fathers, Native Americans, the French, and so on.

As seen in the previous list, we have identified thirteen discrete types of details on which teachers might focus:

1. People

2. Organizations or groups

3. Intellectual or artistic products

4. Naturally occurring objects or animals

5. Naturally occurring places

6. Manmade objects

7. Manmade places

8. Events

9. Natural phenomena

10. Physical actions

11. Mental actions

12. Feelings, conditions, or states

13. Human constructs (ways of organizing the world)

Of course, there is an infinite number of ways to classify details; we simply offer our list of thirteen as a useful organizational scheme that teachers can use to analyze a topic and identify details for questioning. Throughout the book, we identify these types of details in bold text to assist readers' understanding and application of the concepts in their classrooms.

One advantage of our classification scheme is that once a teacher has decided on the type of details to ask questions about, he or she can use the question stems and prompt words in table 2.1 to guide the formulation of detail questions. Prompt words in table 2.1 are shown in italics to further assist teachers as they create questions, but should not be confused with the thirteen types of details (although there is some duplication, such as with people, places, events, and so on). Nor should teachers feel constrained to include the prompt words in every question. For example, the question, When did George Washington live? is a *time period* question about a person, even though it does not include the words "time period."

Table 2.1: Stems for Detail Questions

Type	Detail Questions
People	What *time period* is associated with this person? What *places* are associated with this person? What *events* are associated with this person? What *accomplishments* are associated with this person?
Organizations or groups	What *beliefs* are associated with this organization or group? What *locations* are associated with this organization or group? What *time period* is associated with this organization or group? What *events* are associated with this organization or group?
Intellectual or artistic products	What *person* is associated with this product? What *time period* is associated with this product? What *event* is associated with this product? What *causes or consequences* are associated with this product? What *places* are associated with this product? What *values* are associated with this product?
Naturally occurring objects or animals	What *events* are associated with this object or animal? What *people* are associated with this object or animal? What *time period* is associated with this object or animal? What *locations* are associated with this object or animal? What *system* is this object or animal a part of? What *color, number/quantity, or dimension* is associated with this object or animal?
Naturally occurring places	What *events* are associated with this place? What *people* are associated with this place? What *time period* is associated with this place? What *location* is associated with this place?

Continued on next page →

Type	Detail Questions
Manmade objects	What *locations* are associated with this object? How is this object *used*? What *larger entity* is this object part of? What is the *process* for making this object? What does this object *look like*? What *value* is associated with this object? What *dangers* are associated with this object?
Manmade places	What *events* are associated with this place? What *people* are associated with this place? What *location* is associated with this place? What *actions* are performed at this place? What *larger entity* is this place part of? How is this place *acquired or sold*? What *value* is associated with this place? What *dangers* are associated with this place?
Events	What *people* are associated with this event? What *time period* or date is associated with this event? What *places* are associated with this event? What *causes or consequences* are associated with this event? What *happened* during this event? What *equipment* was used during this event? What *problems* were caused or solved by this event?
Natural phenomena	What *places* are associated with this phenomenon? What *time* is associated with this phenomenon? What *causes or consequences* are associated with this phenomenon? What *happened/happens* during this phenomenon?
Physical actions	What *process* is associated with this physical action? What *locations* are associated with this physical action? What *purpose* is associated with this physical action? What *causes or consequences* are associated with this physical action?
Mental actions	What *process* is associated with this mental action? What *purpose* is associated with this mental action? What *causes or consequences* are associated with this mental action?

Type	Detail Questions
Feelings, conditions, or states	What *actions* are associated with this feeling, condition, or state? What *causes or consequences* are associated with this feeling, condition, or state? What *places* are associated with this feeling, condition, or state? What *values* are associated with this feeling, condition, or state? How does something or someone *arrive at* this feeling, condition, or state? What *dangers* are associated with this feeling, condition, or state?
Human constructs (ways of organizing the world)	What *concept* does the human construct refer to? What *measurement, quantity, or quality* is associated with the human construct? In what way does the human construct help *organize the world*?

Visit **marzanoresearch.com/classroomstrategies** for a reproducible version of this table.

It is important to note that not every question stem in table 2.1 will apply to every detail that is the focus of a questioning sequence. As illustrated in examples throughout the book and in appendix B (page 97), teachers should select those question stems from table 2.1 that are most helpful in eliciting appropriate information from students about details relevant to the questioning sequence.

To illustrate how table 2.1 might be used, assume that a teacher has decided to focus on **people** of the American Revolution. He applies the questions in the **people** row of table 2.1 to each individual he wants to highlight. For example, to focus on George Washington, he asks the following:

- What *time period* is associated with George Washington?

- What *places* are associated with George Washington?

- What *events* are associated with George Washington?

- What *accomplishments* are associated with George Washington?

He follows his questions about George Washington with these same questions about Thomas Jefferson.

Essentially, each of the **people** questions in table 2.1 becomes a jumping-off place to explore details related to a specific person. Sometimes, students will need to consult external resources to find answers to these types of detail questions. In chapter 3, we discuss how teachers can structure students' use of external resources. The following vignette illustrates a teacher using detail questions in the classroom.

> Mrs. Smith has just previewed information about the American Revolutionary War with her class and explained that at the end of the unit, students will be required to assume the character of a man or woman involved in the Revolutionary War, explain the views and perspectives of that character, and answer questions from the class while staying in character. To prepare students for this, Mrs. Smith has designed a questioning sequence that focuses on people of the American Revolution. To find out what students already know about specific Revolutionary War figures, Mrs. Smith asks questions about the time period, places, events, and accomplishments of a wide variety of men and women from the Revolutionary War period. As students answer, Mrs. Smith makes notes about what her students already know and what they have misconceptions about. When one student states that Martha Washington saved her husband's portrait from

the White House when the British burned it, Mrs. Smith takes the opportunity to correct that student's misconception, explaining that the White House wasn't built until 1792, George and Martha Washington never lived in it (although George Washington did help design and build it), and Dolly Madison was the First Lady who saved George Washington's portrait when the White House was burned by the British during the War of 1812.

Phase 2: Category Questions

Once the teacher has identified a focus for the questioning sequence and asked students questions about details, he asks students questions about categories that the details fit into. To continue the American Revolution example from phase 1, George Washington and Thomas Jefferson both fit into several categories: Founding Fathers, U.S. presidents, slave owners, intellectuals, and so on.

Teachers can select any category that a detail fits into, depending on their instructional goals. For example, if the learning goal for a unit specifies that students study the people of the American Revolution, with an emphasis on those who became U.S. presidents and first ladies, U.S. presidents would be an excellent category to use during this phase of the questioning sequence. Alternatively, if the learning goal specified that students study the ideas behind the American Revolution, with an emphasis on intellectual leaders in America at that time, the teacher might focus on the category of intellectuals in colonial and revolutionary America. If the teacher's learning goal required students to learn about people of the American Revolution, with an emphasis on the merchants, landholders, and entrepreneurs of the time, he might focus on the category of colonial American businessmen. The questioning sequence described in this book is flexible enough to allow teachers to align questioning sequences closely to their learning goals and target outcomes for any unit. Suffice it to say that the category a teacher selects becomes the focal point of a questioning sequence. Therefore, it should be done thoughtfully.

For the purposes of illustration, assume that the teacher has selected U.S. presidents as the category he will focus on during the second phase of the questioning sequence. There are three types of category questions that teachers can use: (1) asking students to identify examples in a category, (2) asking students to describe the general characteristics of a category, and (3) asking students to make comparisons within and across categories.

Identify Examples in a Category

These types of questions are designed to help students think of multiple examples that fit in the selected category. Generating additional examples serves to more clearly define the category itself and prepares students to make generalizations about general characteristics of the category. If students had already answered detail questions about George Washington and Thomas Jefferson, and the teacher asked them to generate additional examples that fit in the category of U.S. presidents, students might give the following examples:

- John Adams

- Bill Clinton

- George W. Bush

- Barack Obama

The teacher should encourage students to generate as many examples as possible that fit in the designated category (we review specific strategies for eliciting multiple examples from students in chapter 4).

Once students have generated a robust list of examples that fit in a category, they examine those examples to identify what they have in common. These commonalities are considered to be general characteristics of the category.

Describe the General Characteristics of a Category

These types of questions are designed to help students identify common characteristics that they associate with all examples in a category. As explained previously, the easiest way for students to do this is to examine the list of examples they generated and find commonalities between the examples. For example, by examining a list of U.S. presidents, students might conclude that U.S. presidents tend to have the following characteristics:

- They are powerful.

- They are men.

- They are American citizens.

Teachers can help students identify more characteristics by asking further questions. The question stems in table 2.2 could be used by the teacher to prompt students to generate additional characteristics. As with the detail questions in table 2.1 (pages 17–19), prompt words for each stem are shown in italics.

Table 2.2: Stems for Category Questions

Type	Category Questions
People	What *actions* do people in this category perform?
	What are *requirements* to become someone in this category?
	What *physical traits* are common among people in this category?
	What *psychological traits* are common to people in this category?
Organizations or groups	What *purpose* is associated with organizations or groups in this category?
	What *people* are associated with organizations or groups in this category?
	What *places* are associated with organizations or groups in this category?
Intellectual or artistic products	What *process* is associated with products in this category?
	What *purpose* or use is associated with products in this category?
	What *people* are associated with products in this category?
Naturally occurring objects or animals	What *places* are associated with objects or animals in this category?
	What *physical traits* are associated with objects or animals in this category?
	What *uses* are associated with objects or animals in this category?
Naturally occurring places	What *locations* are associated with places in this category?
	What *physical traits* are associated with places in this category?
	How are places in this category *formed*?
	What *uses* are associated with places in this category?

Continued on next page →

Type	Category Questions
Manmade objects	What *places* are associated with objects in this category? What *physical traits* are associated with objects in this category? How are objects in this category *built or made*? What *uses* are associated with objects in this category? What *dangers* are presented by objects in this category?
Manmade places	What *locations* are associated with places in this category? What *physical traits* are associated with places in this category? How are places in this category *built*? What *uses* are associated with places in this category? What *dangers* are presented by places in this category?
Events	What *people* are associated with events in this category? What *processes or actions* are associated with events in this category? What *equipment, materials, or resources* are associated with events in this category? What *places* are associated with events in this category? What *causes and consequences* are associated with events in this category?
Natural phenomena	What *process* is associated with phenomena in this category? What *causes or consequences* are associated with phenomena in this category? What *places* are associated with phenomena in this category?
Physical actions	What *process* is associated with physical actions in this category? What *locations* are associated with physical actions in this category? What *purpose* is associated with physical actions in this category? What *causes or consequences* are associated with physical actions in this category?
Mental actions	What *process* is associated with mental actions in this category? What *locations* are associated with mental actions in this category? What *causes or consequences* are associated with mental actions in this category?
Feelings, conditions, or states	What are the *causes or consequences* of feelings, conditions, or states in this category? What *process* is involved in reaching feelings, conditions, or states in this category?
Human constructs (ways of organizing the world)	What *purpose* or use is associated with human constructs in this category? What *causes or consequences* are associated with human constructs in this category?

Visit **marzanoresearch.com/classroomstrategies** for a reproducible version of this table.

As with the stems in table 2.1 (pages 17–19), teachers should note that not every stem in table 2.2 will apply to every category that is the focus of a questioning sequence. As shown in examples throughout the book and in appendix B (page 97), teachers should select those stems that are most helpful in eliciting the characteristics of their focus category or categories. Using the question stems in table 2.2 for categories of **people**, the teacher might ask:

- What *actions* do U.S. presidents perform?

- What are *requirements* to become a U.S. president?

- What *physical traits* are common to U.S. presidents?

- What *psychological traits* are common to U.S. presidents?

In response to these specific category questions, students might generate additional characteristics for the category of U.S. presidents such as *lead the nation*, *sign bills into law*, *veto bills*, *represent the nation*, *must be elected*, *must be thirty-five or older*, *must be a natural-born American citizen*, *men*, *tall*, and *good communicators*. Referring back to the stimulus questions derived from table 2.2, the first four answers are about actions U.S. presidents perform, the next three are requirements to be a U.S. president, the next two are physical traits of U.S. presidents, and the last is a psychological trait of U.S. presidents. By using the guidance provided in table 2.2, teachers can help students go beyond their initial thoughts and explore characteristics of a category on a deeper level.

Make Comparisons Within and Across Categories

The final type of question a teacher might ask about categories involves comparing examples within the same category as well as from different categories. These comparisons help students identify characteristics that are unique to a category and those that are shared between several categories. For example, the teacher asks students to compare George Washington to Barack Obama (same category of U.S. presidents). Students observe that Washington and Obama both served two terms as president (similarity), that Washington is generally considered to have been an introvert while Obama is generally considered to be an extrovert (difference), that they both published books (similarity), and that Obama's book was read by many more people than Washington's (difference). These observations can also prompt students to examine how the role of U.S. presidents has changed since the 18th century.

For an across-category comparison, the teacher asks students to compare George Washington to Mohammed Morsi (one is in the category of U.S. presidents, the other is in the category of foreign presidents). Students observe that while George Washington was reluctant to be president, did not grab for power while he was president, and stepped down after two terms because he did not want to seek re-election (although he could have, according to the laws of his time), Mohammed Morsi seemed interested in getting power, consolidating power, and staying in power as long as possible. They also observe that George Washington became president of a country that had just rebelled against an outside ruler (King George of England), whereas Mohammed Morsi became president of a country that had just rebelled against its own ruler (Hosni Mubarak of Egypt). These comparisons can help students become aware of the unique challenges and successes of future American presidents during the Revolutionary War time period.

In addition to allowing students to express similarities and differences, across-category comparisons can be extended by inviting students to identify a new category into which both examples fit. For example, George Washington and Mohammed Morsi both fit into the category of first president of a country. Students can extend their thinking by creating generalizations about this new category, if time allows and it is appropriate to the content.

As students generate examples, characteristics, and similarities and differences for categories, they are continuing the work begun during the detail phase: surfacing and making explicit information that they will use to make elaborations about the content during the third phase of the questioning sequence. The following vignette illustrates how a teacher can lead students during the category phase.

Mrs. Smith moves her students into the category phase of questioning by suggesting three categories of people from the American Revolution: (1) future presidents, (2) businessmen, and (3) intellectuals. She asks students to pick the category they are most interested in and work with others who have chosen that category to generate examples and characteristics of people in that category. Seven students decide to investigate American intellectuals in the 18th century. They identify Benjamin Franklin, Thomas Jefferson, John Adams, James Madison, and other intellectuals highlighted during the detail phase.

Students point out that some of these individuals fit into the other categories, and Mrs. Smith explains that this is okay, saying, "Your goal is to identify intellectuals during the 18th century, and the examples you've generated are all in that category. It's okay if they fit into other categories too; in fact, most examples will fit into lots of different categories. That's why you're narrowing your focus to just one category: intellectuals."

Once students have generated examples in their category, they brainstorm general characteristics of the category.

"They're all men," says Sadie.

This observation prompts students to add some female examples, like Mercy Otis Warren and Abigail Adams.

"They all read a lot, and some of them wrote books and papers," says Meisha.

Mrs. Smith asks the group specific questions to prompt them to brainstorm further, such as, What actions did intellectuals perform in the 18th century? and What psychological traits were common for 18th century intellectuals? After students have compiled a list of characteristics, Mrs. Smith asks questions that prompt students to compare 18th century intellectuals to intellectuals from other time periods, such as: How were the ideas of Benjamin Franklin and Niccolò Machiavelli similar and different? How were the ideas of Benjamin Franklin and John Locke similar and different? How were the ideas of Benjamin Franklin and Karl Marx similar and different? Mrs. Smith asks students to specifically compare intellectuals' views of government, power, and the responsibilities of the leaders and citizens. As students answer the comparison questions, they realize that ideas about how government should derive its power and the responsibilities of the people of a country changed dramatically in the 18th century, largely due to thinkers like John Locke and Thomas Paine.

Phase 3: Elaboration Questions

The third phase of a questioning sequence involves asking students to elaborate on characteristics they identified during the category phase. Elaboration questions (and phase 4: evidence questions) are particularly important in developing students' abilities to make and defend claims, a process often referred to as *argumentation*. Creating claims and defending them with evidence is an important skill highlighted in the Common Core State Standards (CCSS). The authors stated that "students must think critically and deeply, assess the validity of their own thinking, and anticipate counterclaims in opposition to their own assertions" (NGA & CCSSO, 2010b, p. 24). During phase 3 of a questioning sequence, students engage in critical thinking by elaborating on the information surfaced during the first two phases. Three kinds of questions prompt elaboration: (1) asking students to explain reasons for characteristics, (2) asking students to describe the effects of specific characteristics, and (3) asking students to project what might occur under certain conditions.

Explain Reasons for Characteristics

Here, students provide explanations for the characteristics they generated during the second phase of the questioning sequence. These questions are usually formatted as Why? questions. For example, based on the answers students generated during the category phase of questioning about U.S. presidents, the teacher might ask any of the following questions:

- Why are presidents powerful?

- Why are presidents usually men?

- Why are presidents American citizens?

- Why do presidents sign bills into law?

- Why do presidents veto bills?

- Why must presidents be elected?

- Why must presidents be thirty-five or older?

- Why must presidents be natural-born U.S. citizens?

To respond to these questions, students will probably need time to think, look for additional information, and confer with their peers. In chapter 3, we explain how teachers can help students find and interpret the information they need to answer questions, and in chapter 4, we describe specific strategies that teachers can use to facilitate group work and peer interaction during the elaboration phase.

Describe the Effects of Specific Characteristics

This type of elaboration question asks students to describe the effects of characteristics they identified during the category phase of the questioning sequence. For example, assume that students generated the following characteristics about U.S. presidents during the category phase of a questioning sequence:

- They tend to be good communicators.

- They have to be American citizens.

- They have the power to sign or veto bills.

During the elaboration phase, a teacher might ask questions about the effects of those characteristics:

- What effect does being a good communicator have on a president?

- What effect does being an American citizen have on a president?

- What effect does the president's power to sign or veto bills have on the United States?

Again, because elaboration questions require deeper thinking and may involve dialogue, research, or further investigation, students might work in groups to answer them. We explain structures and skills that facilitate groups' thinking and collaboration in chapter 4.

Project What Might Occur Under Certain Conditions

This type of elaboration question usually takes a What if? format and requires students to predict what might happen (or might have happened) under certain conditions. For example, the teacher asks students to project what might have happened if George Washington had died when he contracted smallpox in 1751 or if Thomas Jefferson had abolished slavery.

Like the previous two types of elaboration questions, What If? or projection questions commonly require students to gather information from external sources (see chapter 3) and collaborate with their peers (see chapter 4). Questions like these invariably involve differing opinions between students. Students should seek out these opinions and consider them when formulating their answers. The following vignette illustrates how a teacher can guide her students during the elaboration phase of the questioning sequence.

Mrs. Smith explains that the next phase of the questioning sequence will require students to think more deeply about reasons, effects, and hypothetical outcomes. For each category of people that students investigated, Mrs. Smith designs a series of elaboration questions. To the group investigating 18th century intellectuals, she asks:

- Why were the intellectuals you examined literary people (readers and authors)?

- Why were the intellectuals you examined mainly Caucasian?

- Why were the intellectuals you examined mostly men, or women married to intellectual men?

- What effect does being a literary person have on being an intellectual?

- What effect did being Caucasian in the 18th century have on being an intellectual?

- What effect did being married to an intellectual have on women in the 18th century?

- What if Benjamin Franklin's brother had not been a printer?

Students form pairs or triads, and each group selects one or more of the questions to investigate and answer. Marta and Jessica, who are considering role-playing Abigail Adams and Mercy Otis Warren for their final project, decide to investigate the effects of being married to or related to an intellectual in the 18th century. Among other things, they find that Mercy Otis Warren was the wife and daughter of intellectuals (her husband James served in the Massachusetts state congress and was friends with John Adams; her father was an attorney and judge in Massachusetts) and that Abigail Adams was related to John Hancock's wife; was the daughter of an intellectual minister; was married to John Adams, who became the second U.S. president; and was active in the intellectual culture of the American Revolution.

In contrast, the girls discover that Benjamin Franklin was the son of a soap and candle maker. Although Benjamin's brother James started a printing company, Benjamin was only an apprentice there and wasn't allowed to write for the paper (although he managed to sneak in a few letters under the pseudonym "Mrs. Silence Dogood"). Despite these obstacles, Franklin traveled to Europe, worked in London for a time, and went on to become a statesman and an intellectual leader in the 18th century. His daughter, Sarah Franklin Bache, became an intellectual leader in support of the American colonists during the Revolution. Based on these discoveries, the girls conclude that although men in the 18th century were able to become intellectuals in spite of disadvantages, women often needed to be surrounded and supported by men who were intellectuals to be able to succeed in their pursuit of knowledge.

Phase 4: Evidence Questions

During the evidence phase of the questioning sequence, the teacher asks students to provide support for their elaborations from the previous phase. Often, this requires students to refer back to information they collected or generated during the first three phases of the questioning sequence and may also require additional research and investigation from external sources (see chapter 3). There are five ways a teacher can prompt students to provide support for their elaborations: (1) ask students to identify sources that support their elaborations, (2) ask students to explain the reasoning they used to construct their elaborations, (3) ask students to qualify or restrict some of their conclusions, (4) ask students to find errors in the reasoning used to construct their elaborations, and (5) ask students to examine their elaborations from different perspectives.

Identify Sources That Support Elaborations

One of the simplest ways to elicit evidence is by asking students to name the source of their information. For example, a student might have stated during the elaboration phase that the effect of being an American citizen on a U.S. president is that the president understands the values and beliefs that are important to American citizens. During the evidence phase, the teacher asks the student to list sources that support that elaboration. As one source, the student refers to an academic journal article about a sociological study of citizens' values and beliefs in various countries. Students should ensure that their sources are reliable and credible, especially if they are derived from the Internet.

Explain the Reasoning Used to Construct Elaborations

Teachers can also ask students to explain the reasoning underlying their conclusions and the reasoning process they used to formulate their elaborations. For example, the student who said that being an American citizen helps a president understand the values and beliefs important to Americans might explain his reasoning as follows:

> People who are natural-born American citizens are either born in the United States or born to parents who are both American citizens. If you are born in the United States, you will be exposed to other American citizens as you grow up and will learn what is important to them. You will probably also go to school in the United States, your teachers will be American citizens, and the things they teach will reflect American values and beliefs. If your parents are Americans, but you are born in another country, you will learn about important American values and beliefs from your parents.

Here, the student is explaining the premises from which he formed his conclusion that being an American citizen causes U.S. presidents to be familiar with American values and beliefs. In effect, the credibility of the evidence the student is providing indicates the soundness of his reasoning.

Qualify or Restrict Some Conclusions

When students create elaborations and provide evidence for them, there may be aspects of a question or issue that they fail to consider. Evidence questions that focus on these aspects prompt students to clarify or qualify (explain when it might not be true) their elaborations to incorporate previously unconsidered information. Identifying the restrictions on an elaboration always strengthens one's argument.

For example, the student who said that a being an American citizen helps a president understand American values and beliefs realizes that some children are born in the United States but grow up in foreign countries, and their parents are not American citizens. Based on this consideration, the student clarifies his reasoning to include this particular group of people, explaining,

> In the case of individuals who are American citizens by birth, but who did not grow up in the United States and do not have American parents, they are still allowed to run for president, but it may be difficult for them to get elected since they may not share fundamental beliefs and values with their constituents.

Identifying qualifications or restrictions on their elaborations helps students take a more analytic view toward their own (and others') reasoning. Collaborative discussions with peers can highlight other perspectives that may help students understand how they need to clarify or qualify their answers. In chapter 4, we explain how teachers can set up and structure these discussions.

Find Errors in the Reasoning Used to Construct Elaborations

Here, the teacher asks students to examine their reasoning and elaborations for misleading or inaccurate information. As we explain in chapter 5, there are specific types of errors that students can look for in their reasoning: errors of faulty logic, attack, weak reference, and misinformation. We describe each of these errors in chapter 5 and explain how teachers can prompt students to look for them. If a student observed that presidents are tall because most people think tall people are good leaders, the teacher might ask him how his elaboration could be misleading.

The student responds that his claim contains an error of misinformation: "Well, one of my examples doesn't support my elaboration. James Madison was only five feet four inches tall."

As a follow-up question, the teacher asks, "How could your elaboration be corrected or improved to eliminate confusion?"

The student replies, "The average height in America in the 1800s was shorter than the current average height. Therefore, I could say instead that most presidents are tall compared to the average height of the population."

Examine Elaborations From Different Perspectives

Finally, teachers can ask students to consider their elaborations from other perspectives. For example, a teacher asks a student who said that presidents need to be good communicators in order to get people to follow them, "Why would someone consider your elaboration to be right or wrong?"

The student replies, "Not all people agree about whether different presidents were good communicators. For example, some say that George W. Bush, Nixon, and Eisenhower were not gifted public speakers."

Students should revise their elaborations to address conflicting viewpoints. Teachers can prompt this revision by asking, "How would you respond to that person's perspective?" In this case, the student revises her claim to make a clearer distinction between communicating and public speaking. The following vignette illustrates how a teacher can guide students during the evidence phase of a questioning sequence.

> As Mrs. Smith's students enter the evidence phase of the questioning sequence, she encourages them to re-examine their elaborations and explicitly state support for them. She visits with each small group to help them decide what type of evidence they need to consider. When she

meets with Marta and Jessica, she recognizes that they have already identified the source of their information and the reasoning they used to construct their argument. So, she challenges them to qualify or restrict their conclusion by examining it from a different perspective.

"What about women like Hannah Bostwick McDougall, Esther De Berdt Reed, Deborah Sampson, and Judith Sargent Murray? What were their situations like? Do their stories support or contradict your claim?" Mrs. Smith asks.

The girls do more research and find that Hannah Bostwick McDougall was married to Alexander McDougall, who published a patriot newspaper. Esther De Berdt Reed was married to a lawyer and political leader who served as George Washington's secretary during the American Revolution. These two examples strengthen their conclusion that intellectual women were surrounded and encouraged by intellectual men. However, when they investigate the lives of Deborah Sampson and Judith Sargent Murray, they find some surprising information. Deborah Sampson, known for disguising herself as a man and fighting in the American Revolution, grew up poor and was abandoned by her father when she was young, forcing her to become an indentured servant.

"Okay, so she wasn't surrounded by intellectuals. But I'm not sure I would call her an intellectual," says Marta. "More like a really brave woman who was willing to endure a lot of hardship for her country."

"So, she doesn't really fit as an example of someone in our category," replies Jessica.

The girls find out that Judith Sargent Murray was raised by parents who didn't allow her to study the classics or other educational subjects because she wasn't a boy. She grew up to be a strong advocate for women's rights and wrote multiple books, essays, and letters.

"She's an exception," says Jessica.

"Yeah," says Marta. "She wasn't really surrounded by intellectuals or encouraged to be an intellectual, but she became one herself."

The girls decide to modify their claim to include a qualifier that says that although many intellectual women in the 18th century were surrounded by male intellectuals who supported and encouraged them, some women, such as Judith Sargent Murray, successfully sought out education and learning even without male support.

Flexibility With Questioning Sequences

In this chapter we have presented the four phases of a questioning sequence and the various forms each phase can take. There are many options within each phase. These constitute a system that can have a variety of manifestations. This is depicted in figure 2.2 (page 30).

As figure 2.2 indicates, a teacher can move within each of the four phases of a questioning sequence in a variety of ways. While teachers move from one phase to the next in a linear fashion (detail, category, elaboration, evidence), each phase provides many options for teachers and students alike. Depending on the selections a teacher makes from the options outlined in figure 2.2, a questioning sequence can span multiple days or be conducted completely within a single class period. In chapter 5, we consider how planning differs for short versus extended questioning sequences.

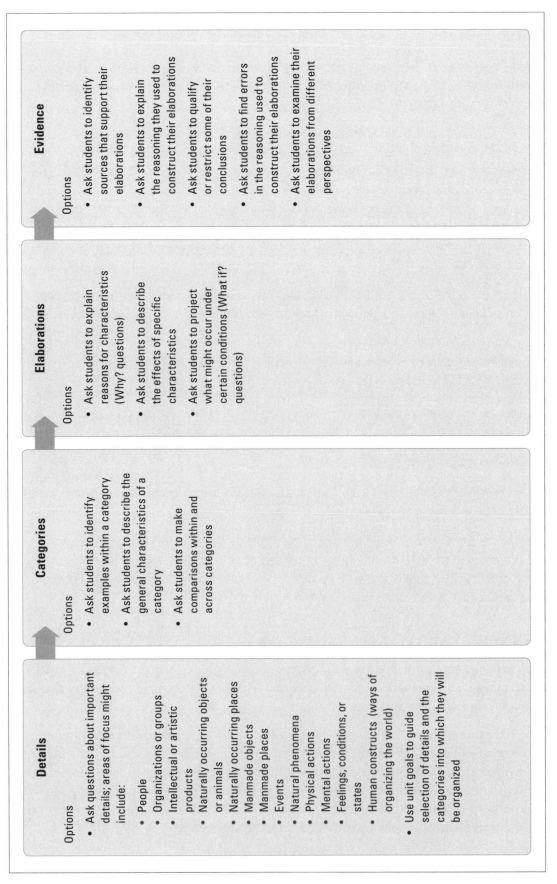

Details

Options

- Ask questions about important details; areas of focus might include:
  - People
  - Organizations or groups
  - Intellectual or artistic products
  - Naturally occurring objects or animals
  - Naturally occurring places
  - Manmade objects
  - Manmade places
  - Events
  - Natural phenomena
  - Physical actions
  - Mental actions
  - Feelings, conditions, or states
  - Human constructs (ways of organizing the world)
- Use unit goals to guide selection of details and the categories into which they will be organized

Categories

Options

- Ask students to identify examples within a category
- Ask students to describe the general characteristics of a category
- Ask students to make comparisons within and across categories

Elaborations

Options

- Ask students to explain reasons for characteristics (Why? questions)
- Ask students to describe the effects of specific characteristics
- Ask students to project what might occur under certain conditions (What if? questions)

Evidence

Options

- Ask students to identify sources that support their elaborations
- Ask students to explain the reasoning they used to construct their elaborations
- Ask students to qualify or restrict some of their conclusions
- Ask students to find errors in the reasoning used to construct their elaborations
- Ask students to examine their elaborations from different perspectives

Figure 2.2: Options within the phases of a questioning sequence.

Visit **marzanoresearch.com/classroomstrategies** for a reproducible version of this figure.

Summary

The questioning sequence explained in this chapter is a structure that teachers can use to plan and implement effective questioning sequences in their classrooms. Unlike previous guidance given to teachers about asking questions, our questioning sequence embraces all "levels" of questions, acknowledging that each has its proper place and is very powerful when used in the right way at the right time. As mentioned previously, it is unlikely that students will already know all the information necessary to answer questions during the four phases of the questioning sequence based on prior knowledge or experience alone. In many cases, they will have to seek information from outside resources and texts. In chapter 3, we describe a wide variety of these texts and explain how teachers can prepare students to interact with them to secure the information they need.

Chapter 2: Comprehension Questions

1. Why are detail questions so important to the questioning sequence? What is the most important consideration when designing detail questions?

2. During the category phase, how should teachers select appropriate categories for questioning sequences?

3. How is the argumentation process incorporated into the elaboration and evidence phases of a questioning sequence?

4. What should students be able to explain about their elaborations or conclusions during the evidence phase?

Chapter 3

EXTERNAL SOURCES OF INFORMATION

Students have two sources of information with which to answer questions: their prior knowledge and external sources. When students have the requisite prior knowledge to answer a question, their response time is quite short, even immediate. When students do not have this knowledge, they must obtain the information elsewhere—from an external source. This can occur during the detail phase but more commonly occurs during the category, elaboration, and evidence phases of the questioning sequence. For example, consider the following category question: What are examples of stars that are G-type main sequence stars?

Students might have to search for examples externally unless they are very familiar with G-type main sequence stars. Now consider the following elaboration question: What effect does nuclear fusion have on G-type main sequence stars?

Again, students will typically need to search for new information in external sources to answer this type of question. Similarly, consider the following evidence question: Do G-type main sequence stars ever not become red giants when they exhaust all of their hydrogen?

Whenever students must go beyond their knowledge base to answer a question, it is important for the teacher to facilitate the process by helping them understand the characteristics of the external sources they consult. In this chapter, we describe how teachers can help students understand and glean useful information from three general types of external information: (1) linguistic texts, (2) nonlinguistic texts, and (3) electronic texts.

Linguistic Texts

Linguistic texts are traditional texts: printed letters organized into words, sentences, and paragraphs. Researchers postulate that traditional linguistic texts have three levels of meaning: (1) top-level structures, (2) subordinate structures, and (3) details. Details can relate to subordinate structures or directly to top-level structures. Figure 3.1 (page 34) illustrates this organization.

Top-level structures are used to organize an entire text. For example, the following text uses a top-level description structure (see table 3.1 on page 35 for additional types of text structures):

> Orca, or killer, whales are the largest members of the dolphin family. They live in small, close-knit pods. To communicate with each other, orcas use a combination of clicks, whistles, and calls. Orcas grow to about thirty feet in length and weigh about ten thousand pounds. They have characteristic

markings: mostly black with white patches and a white belly. Orca whales are top predators (their only enemy is humans) and eat a varied diet of fish, squid, sharks, marine mammals, turtles, and birds. Orcas are found in all of the world's oceans and most of its seas.

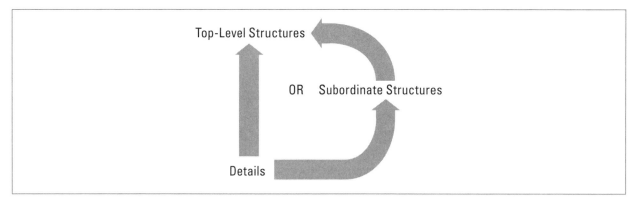

Figure 3.1: Levels of meaning in linguistic texts.

Description structures involve listing the characteristics or attributes of something—in this case, orca whales. Texts can also contain subordinate structures. For example, the third sentence in the previous text contains a subordinate problem/solution structure: orcas need to communicate with each other (problem), so they use a combination of clicks, whistles, and calls (solution). Finally, texts always contain details. Each sentence in the passage about orcas contains one or more details such as orcas are members of the dolphin family; orcas live in small, close-knit pods; and orcas grow to thirty feet.

Top-level and subordinate structures organize the details in a text by relating them to each other in specific ways. In the following sections, we describe five different types of structures found in texts and discuss how students can use those structures to look for specific information in texts, understand and interpret texts, and remember the information they find in texts. We then discuss how students can identify top-level and subordinate structures. These skills are critical for students to have as they seek and interpret information from external sources during questioning sequences.

Text Structures

Structures are critical to understanding what is expressed in linguistic texts. They allow people to expect, seek, and organize specific information from a text in their memories. Kintsch (1988) stated that "people understand correctly because they sort of know what is going to come" (p. 164). Peter Mosenthal and Irwin Kirsch (1991a) further explained,

> By knowing what types of information to expect for each document type, we minimize surprises when we encounter new documents and we have a ready set of categories for understanding the data and details of even the most complex documents. (p. 655)

Essentially, text structures are like blank organizers that readers mentally fill in as they read a text. Structures facilitate comprehension by letting the reader know what details are important to look for and how they can expect the ideas in a text to relate to each other. Understanding text structures and using them to interrelate the ideas in a text will not only help students better understand what they read but will also improve their memory and retention of what they read.

Bonnie Meyer, Carole Young, and Brendan Bartlett (1989) identified five structures that can be used to classify all linguistic texts: (1) description, (2) sequence, (3) causation, (4) problem/solution, and (5) comparison. Each structure is described in table 3.1, along with the signal words and phrases that indicate its use.

Table 3.1: Text Structures With Their Signal Words and Phrases

Text Structure	Signal Words and Phrases
Description structures enumerate attributes, specifics, or setting information about a topic. For example, a descriptive passage about monkeys might describe the physical characteristics of monkeys, one particular type of monkey, the environment of monkeys, and so on. Newspaper articles often use a descriptive plan, telling about who, where, how, and when.	*attributes of, characteristics are, for example, for instance, in describing, marks of, namely, properties of, qualities are, specifically, such as, that is, this particular, which was one*
Sequence structures group ideas based on order or time. A number of items are ordered in a continuous progression related to a particular topic. Recipes often follow a sequence structure, explaining which ingredients should be added first, next, then, and last. Historical accounts and stories also typically use sequence structures.	*after, afterwards, as time passed, before, continuing on, early, finally, following, in the first place, last, later, more recently, soon, to begin with, to end, years ago*
Causation structures present ideas in cause-and-effect relationships. Directions typically follow a causation sequence: if you want a certain outcome (effect), then follow these steps (cause). Explanations of a particular event may also follow causation structures, explaining the reasons or causes behind it.	*as a result, because, caused, consequence, consequently, for the purpose of, if/then, in explanation, in order to, led to, since, so, the reason, therefore, this is why, thus*
Problem/Solution structures organize ideas into two main parts: problem and solution. Texts that feature questions and answers often follow problem/solution structures. For example, a scientific article raises a problem or question and then seeks to provide a solution or answer to the question.	*answer, comeback, enigma, issue, need to prevent, perplexity, problem, puzzle, query, question, rejoinder, reply, response, return, riddle, solution, the trouble, to satisfy the problem, to set the issue at rest, to solve these problems*
Comparison structures relate ideas to each other on the basis of their similarities and differences. These can be simple (comparing different brands of laundry detergent) or more complex (comparing beliefs about God or legal arguments). Sometimes an author will present both sides of an issue without recommending one over the other. Other times, as in political speeches, one side of the issue will be portrayed as correct and the other side as incorrect.	*act like, alike, all but, although, but, compare to, difference, different, differentiate, have in common, however, in comparison, in contrast, in opposition, instead, not everyone, on the other hand, resemble, share, the same as, unlike, whereas, while*

Source: Adapted from Meyer et al., 1989.

Visit **marzanoresearch.com/classroomstrategies** for a reproducible version of this table.

In their research, Meyer and her colleagues found that students who identified and used the structures in table 3.1 to organize their reading and recall of texts remembered more from their reading than students who did not use the structures. Similarly, Teun van Dijk and Walter Kintsch's (1983) research indicated that students who identified the organizational structures that a text suggested remembered the text better than those who simply tried to remember a list of facts from the text.

To identify text structures, students can look for signal words and phrases. For instance, if a student notices *for example, specifically, such as, attributes of, namely*, and so on in a passage of text, the structure of that portion of the text is likely to be descriptive, and the student should look for and remember attributes or characteristics listed in the text as the important details of that part of the text. If words such as *afterwards, later, finally, first, last, following, before, after*, and so on are used, the structure of the text is likely to be sequential, and the student should pay attention to the order of events in the text as the important details. Similarly, causation, problem/solution, and comparison structures have key words that signal their structures and important details (as shown in table 3.1, page 35). Each of the five structures can also contain list structures embedded within the top-level structure. For example, a sequence may contain a list of ideas ordered sequentially. A causation structure might include lists of causes and effects, comparison structures might include lists of ideas that are contrasted with each other, and so on. Students should be aware that lists occur frequently, and are used within each of the five top-level structures.

Top-Level and Subordinate Structures

Shorter texts are often organized using only one type of structure. Advertisements are excellent examples. A commercial for a sports car might be descriptive, telling about all the features of the car. A movie trailer might be sequential, telling the story of the movie. An ad for a beauty product might use a causation structure to explain all the reasons why it will improve your looks, and an ad for cat food might use a problem/solution structure to explain how it will remedy your pet's laziness, boredom, and weight gain. Political advertising often uses a comparison structure to contrast the views of one candidate to those of the opposing candidate. Newspaper articles are often descriptive, listing what happened, whom it happened to, where it happened, how it happened, and when it happened. Scientific articles use a problem/solution structure: they tell you what the research question was (the problem) and how it was answered (the solution). Historical accounts usually follow a sequence structure. In effect, then, a single structure from those listed in table 3.1 (page 35) may be the only structure used in a text, particularly if the text is short.

Longer texts, however, usually use two or more of the five structures. As already explained, a listing structure might be used within one of the main structures. Alternatively, the structures themselves may be used within one another. Meyer and her colleagues (1989) explained,

> Many texts will reflect more than one of these basic five plans. For example, folktales contain much description, causation, and events sequenced in time within an overall problem/solution plan where the protagonist confronts and resolves a problem. Folktales may carry an overall comparison plan, such as demonstrating the contrast between good and evil. For example, an Aesop fable about a genie and two woodsmen was comprised of two substories: one about an honest woodsman and the other about a dishonest woodsman. The overall plan for the story was comparison with emphasis on the honest woodsman as explicitly signaled by the author in the moral "Honesty is the best policy." (p. 106)

The use of several structures in the same text can be confusing if students fail to understand that there is usually one overarching top-level structure that organizes a text and other subordinate structures that fit into the top-level structure. The top-level structure is frequently referred to as the main idea of a text. Meyer (1982) stated that "a text is not just a series of sentences or paragraphs precisely because it displays a hierarchy of content, so that some facts (statements, etc.) are superordinate or subordinate to others" (p. 38). The top-level structure is usually the one associated most closely with the topic or main idea of a text. So, an article comparing two views of smoking using a comparison structure (smoking is harmful to your body versus smoking relieves tension) might use a subordinate causation structure to explain how smoking harms your body (lung cancer, high blood pressure, and loss of appetite). Figure 3.2 illustrates how that hierarchy might be arranged.

Teaching students to identify the top-level and subordinate structures of a text is at the heart of Meyer and her colleagues' (1989) strategy for improving students' understanding and memory of traditional texts. They defined successful readers as follows:

They approach text with knowledge about how texts are conventionally organized and a strategy to seek and use the top-level structure in a particular text as an organizational framework to facilitate encoding and retrieval. . . . That is, there is a search for relationships which can subsume all or large chunks of this information and tie it into a summarized comprehensible whole. (p. 8)

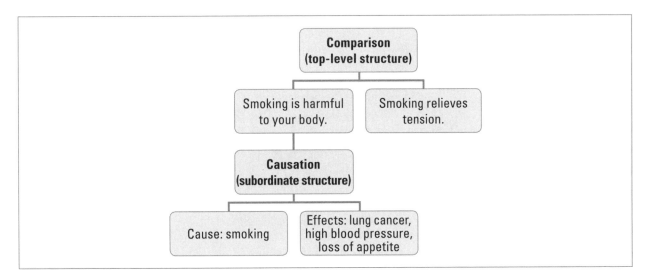

Figure 3.2: Hierarchy of structures in a comparison article about smoking.

Source: Adapted from Meyer et al., 1989.

Meyer suggests that students first learn to identify each of the five structures by examining short passages of text like those described previously. Advertisements, blog posts, encyclopedia articles, and other short segments of text work well for this. After students are familiar with each type of structure, they can read passages, identify the structure, and then try to recall the passage using that structure. So, if a student read a descriptive passage, he or she would look for characteristics or attributes of the thing being described and recall the passage by remembering each of those attributes or characteristics. If a student read a sequential passage, he or she would look for events that occur over time and recall the passage by remembering the order of events. In a causation passage, a student would look for and recall specific causes and effects in the passage. In a problem/solution passage, the student would look for and remember the problem and its solutions, and in a comparison passage, the student would look for and remember information about the items being compared. Essentially, the structure gives the student mental blanks to fill with information as well as prompts to remember that information later. The questions in table 3.2 (page 38) can help students use each text structure.

We recommend the following for teachers to acquaint students with linguistic texts.

1. Teach students about the five text structures and the signal words that correspond to each one.

2. Give students short passages of text or advertisements that use only one structure. Ask them to identify the top-level structure of each text.

3. Ask students to evaluate longer passages of text that contain subordinate structures within a top-level structure. Ask students to diagram the top-level structure and subordinate structures (as shown in figure 3.2).

4. Ask students to use their knowledge of structures to focus on the main ideas as they read a passage. If the passage is mainly descriptive, students should focus on each characteristic or attribute of the item being described. If it is sequential, students should focus on the events in order. For causation passages, students should focus on the cause and its effect. For

problem/solution structures, students should focus on the problem and its solution, and for comparison structures, students should focus on the two items being compared and their similarities and differences.

5. Ask students to retell passages, using the specific information they remember related to their structures.

Table 3.2: Text Structure Questions

Text Structure	Questions
Description	What is being described? What are the important characteristics of the thing being described?
Sequence	What larger event or occurrence is being recounted? What smaller events make up the larger event or occurrence? What order do the smaller events occur in?
Causation	What is the effect being described? What caused the effect? How are the causes related?
Problem/Solution	What is the problem being described? What is the solution or solutions being suggested?
Comparison	What two things are being compared? How are they similar? How are they different?

Visit **marzanoresearch.com/classroomstrategies** for a reproducible version of this table.

The following vignette depicts how a teacher can facilitate students' use of linguistic texts to answer questions.

Mrs. McGould's students have just learned about the five structures of linguistic texts.

"Take a look at the signal words for each text, and then decide what structure this television ad is using," she directs them.

She plays a TV commercial that shows a cell phone being covered in baby food, doused in coffee, smeared with flour, caked with sand, and soaked in the ocean, a swimming pool, a sprinkler, a goldfish bowl, the tire splash from a passing car, and champagne. Each time, the phone is simply rinsed, brushed off, or dried. The tagline is "Whatever-proof" (AT&T, 2013). When the ad is finished, students confer with a partner.

Lesley says, "I'm saying it's problem/solution."

"Yeah," says her partner Mary. "The problem is that most cell phones break when you get them wet or dirty, and the solution is to buy this phone, which can handle all that stuff."

Most of the other students agree, and Mrs. McGould moves on to a print ad from a magazine. For practice with longer texts, Mrs. McGould asks students to read a passage about the causes of the Arab Spring. Although the title makes it fairly obvious that the passage's top-level structure is causation, Mrs. McGould asks her students to focus on substructures within the causation structure. After students finish reading, she records the substructures that students found on the board and then asks students to construct diagrams that show how the substructures fit together and are unified by the overall causation structure.

Nonlinguistic Texts

Whereas linguistic texts primarily use words arranged into sentences and paragraphs to communicate information, nonlinguistic texts primarily use charts, tables, pictures, or other graphics to communicate information. Similar to linguistic texts, nonlinguistic texts adhere to specific structures. As students reference external nonlinguistic texts during questioning sequences, those who are familiar with the different text structures and know what types of information each typically represents will be more likely to understand and remember information they encounter in those texts. Mosenthal and Kirsch (1989a, 1989b, 1990a, 1990b, 1990c, 1990d, 1991a, 1991b, 1991c, 1992; Kirsch & Mosenthal, 1989, 1990a, 1990b, 1990c, 1991, 1992) identified and described a number of specific structures for nonlinguistic texts. We present these structures in three categories: (1) matrix texts (lists and tables), (2) graphic texts (charts and graphs), and (3) mimetic texts (pictures and schematics).

Matrix Texts

According to Mosenthal and Kirsch (1989a, 1989b; Kirsch & Mosenthal, 1989, 1990c), matrix texts are the building blocks of most collections of information. They include simple lists, combined lists, intersected lists, and nested lists. It is likely that students will encounter each of these types of matrix texts as they seek and interpret information in external sources. For example, in response to a detail question about which American colonies existed in 1740, students might look at an external source that contains the simple list in table 3.3.

Table 3.3: Simple List—American Colonies in 1740

American Colonies in 1740		
Connecticut	New Hampshire	Pennsylvania
Delaware	New Jersey	Rhode Island
Georgia	New York	South Carolina
Maryland	North Carolina	Virginia
Massachusetts		

Source: U.S. Bureau of the Census, 1975.

As seen in table 3.3, simple lists consist of a number of items with something in common. The heading at the top of the list alerts the reader to how the items are related. When looking at simple lists, students should try to discover the shared feature that unites the items in a list. In table 3.3, the shared feature is stated clearly in the list heading: American Colonies in 1740. Simple lists may include words, numbers, or pictures. However, the amount of information in a simple list is rather limited. To express more information, combined lists are often used.

A combined list consists of two or more simple lists placed next to each other so that corresponding information is aligned. Students trying to answer a detail question about the populations of the

American colonies in 1740 might encounter the combined list in table 3.4. Notice that it uses words and numbers to give more information than the simple list.

Table 3.4: Combined List—Populations of American Colonies in 1740

Colony	Population in 1740	Colony	Population in 1740
Georgia	2,021	New York	63,665
Delaware	19,870	Pennsylvania	85,637
New Hampshire	23,256	Connecticut	89,580
Rhode Island	25,255	Maryland	116,093
South Carolina	45,000	Massachusetts	151,613
New Jersey	51,373	Virginia	180,440
North Carolina	51,760		

Source: U.S. Bureau of the Census, 1975.

Here, the combined list specifies the population of each colony. Simple and combined lists are often organized in specific ways. The simple list in table 3.3 (page 39) is organized alphabetically. The combined list in table 3.4 is organized according to the population of each colony, from the lowest population (Georgia) at the beginning to the highest population (Virginia) at the end. Lists could also be organized chronologically. If a student were looking for information about colonial imports and exports, he or she might encounter a chronological combined list like the one in table 3.5.

To interpret this type of combined list, students would need to understand that each column contains a category of information (denoted in the header for each column) and that each row gives the value of exports for a specific year and region.

Table 3.5: Combined List—Values of Colonial Exports by Region and Year

Year	Region	Exports	Year	Region	Exports	Year	Region	Exports
1710	New England	£31,112	1740	New England	£72,389	1770	New England	£148,011
1710	Middle colonies	£9,480	1740	Middle colonies	£36,546	1770	Middle colonies	£97,991
1710	Southern colonies	£209,227	1740	Southern colonies	£599,481	1770	Southern colonies	£769,533

Source: U.S. Bureau of the Census, 1975.

Combined lists can display any amount of information through the addition of columns and rows. However, Kirsch and Mosenthal (1989) pointed out that combined lists quickly become redundant as they include more and more information. In table 3.5, for example, entries in the *Year* and *Region* columns occur multiple times, so comparing data by year or region can become inefficient. For that reason, intersecting lists are often used to display data with repeating elements in one or more of the lists. Instead of table 3.5, students seeking an answer to a teacher's question about colonial exports might find a list like the one in table 3.6.

Table 3.6: Intersecting List—Values of Colonial Exports by Region and Year

Year	New England	Middle Colonies	Southern Colonies
1710	£31,112	£9,480	£209,227
1740	£72,389	£36,546	£599,481
1770	£148,011	£97,991	£769,533

Source: U.S. Bureau of the Census, 1975.

As seen in table 3.6, intersecting lists use a more succinct format to provide information. As they read external sources, students should recognize intersecting lists, understand that they are read slightly differently than other types of lists, and be able to interpret the information they contain.

One drawback of intersecting lists is that they can only contain one type of information. In table 3.6, that information is "values of colonial exports." To express more than one type of information, a nested list is needed. Nested lists use series of intersecting lists to present information on multiple topics. Table 3.7 shows an example of a nested list.

Table 3.7: Nested List—Values of Colonial Exports and Imports by Region and Year

Year	Exports			Imports		
	New England	Middle Colonies	Southern Colonies	New England	Middle Colonies	Southern Colonies
1710	£31,112	£9,480	£209,227	£106,338	£40,069	£147,252
1740	£72,389	£36,546	£599,481	£171,081	£175,528	£466,773
1770	£148,011	£97,991	£769,533	£394,451	£610,872	£920,248

Source: U.S. Bureau of the Census, 1975.

Here, it is important for students to remain aware of which section of the list they are consulting. This nested list allows for the display of two types of information: exports and imports. However, nested lists can be extended to display as much information as is necessary.

We recommend the following for teachers to acquaint students with important information about matrix texts.

1. Teach students about the types of matrix texts, using the previous examples (or others like them). Point out the following important features of matrix texts:

   • Information in matrix texts is ordered vertically and horizontally. Labels show which information is represented in rows and which is represented in columns.

- Information in matrix texts can be ordered chronologically, alphabetically, geographically, or using some other ordering scheme. Identifying the ordering scheme will help one understand the information better.

- Most information in matrix texts can be interpreted into a sentence format. For example, a combined list of available cruises might show sailing dates, durations of trips, destinations, and prices. One row of the matrix could be read, "A three-day cruise to the Bahamas departs on November 24 and costs $700." Reading matrix texts using this type of sentence format can help one understand the information more clearly and compare it more easily.

2. Ask students to find examples of different types of matrix texts in print or online sources and bring copies to class.

3. Ask students to sort the matrix texts they found into different types (such as simple lists, combined lists, intersecting lists, and nested lists).

4. Ask questions that prompt students to find specific information in various matrix texts. For example, a student brings in a nested list showing the number of viewers who watched various television shows on different dates, and the teacher asks, "How many viewers watched *Monday Night Football* between October 1 and November 1?"

5. Ask students to find important features of different types of lists (row and column headings, specific topics in nested lists, and so on) and to evaluate the effectiveness of various lists.

The following vignette depicts how a teacher can facilitate students' exploration and use of matrix texts to answer questions.

Mr. Janus has asked his students to find examples of lists in the newspaper, online, in magazines, in books, and in advertising. Jyree brings in a list he cut out of his dad's finance magazine. It shows home prices over the past ten years. Ricia brings in a list of ingredients for a recipe from her mom's cookbook. Lynne found a list online that showed the top ten songs played on the radio that week.

Mr. Janus's students sort their examples into simple lists, combined lists, intersecting lists, and nested lists. Mr. Janus designates a different corner of the room for each type of list, places all the collected examples of each kind of list in their designated corners, and then asks students to choose a corner. When students reach their corner, they work with the other students there to identify what information is displayed horizontally and vertically on each list, and how that information is ordered. Mr. Janus then asks each corner to use one of their lists to create three sentences that express the information from the list. After each corner shares their sentences, students rotate to a new corner and repeat the process. After three rotations, students have explored all of the different types of matrix texts.

To close the activity, Mr. Janus asks category and elaboration questions about the matrix texts that students found. For example, he asks Lynne, "What do all of the top ten songs have in common?" and he asks Ricia, "What basic process is associated with all recipes?" Based on their answers to these category questions, Mr. Janus formulates elaboration questions, asking students to explain why the characteristics they identify are indicative of a specific category of matrix texts.

Graphic Texts

In addition to matrix texts, students will almost certainly encounter graphic texts as they seek information in external sources during questioning sequences. Graphic texts include charts, graphs, and maps. Mosenthal and Kirsch (1990a, 1990b, 1990c, 1990d) reviewed four different kinds of graphic texts: pie charts, bar graphs, line graphs, and maps. Lists of information are often presented as or translated into graphic texts. For example, a student looking for information about the populations of the American colonies during the Revolutionary War period might find a pie chart like the one in figure 3.3 instead of a simple or combined list like the ones from tables 3.3 (page 39) and 3.4 (page 40), respectively.

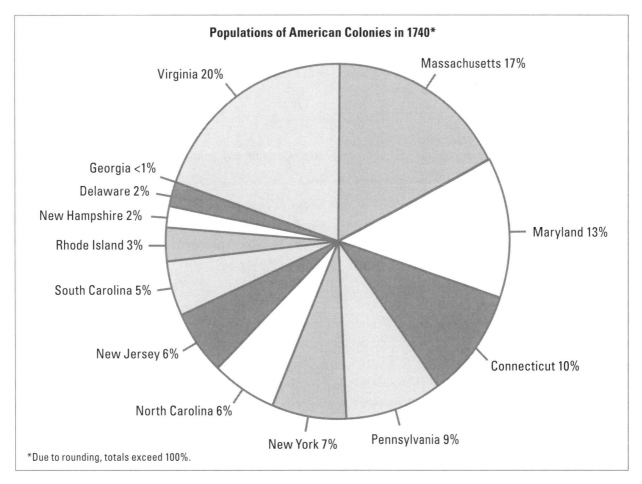

Figure 3.3: Pie chart showing populations of American colonies in 1740.

Source: U.S. Bureau of the Census, 1975.

Pie charts are useful for making comparisons or for immediately identifying important characteristics. For example, showing information about the colonies' populations in a pie chart emphasizes the idea that about half of the colonists lived in Virginia, Massachusetts, and Maryland more forcefully than the same information presented in a list. Students should be aware of this and recognize that authors may choose to present information in a pie chart rather than a list because they want to influence readers in a certain way.

Although pie charts are a useful type of graphic text, they have some drawbacks. Each pie chart can represent only one aspect of information, and the data must be presented as a percentage of the whole. For example, to represent the information about colonial exports from the intersecting list in table 3.6 (page 41), three separate pie charts are necessary, as shown in figure 3.4 (page 44).

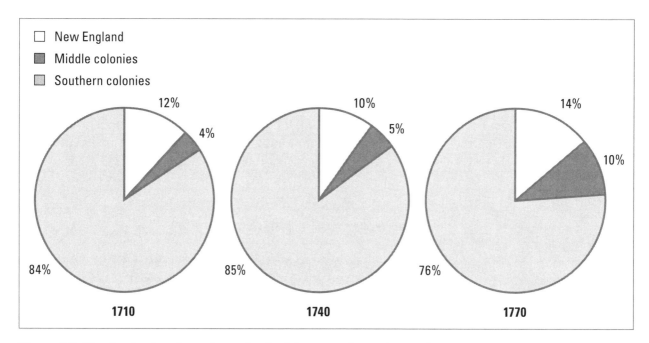

Figure 3.4: Pie charts showing values of colonial exports by region and year.

Source: U.S. Bureau of the Census, 1975.

Here, the pie charts express the value of each region's exports as a percentage of all the exports during a certain year. Although this information is helpful, these charts do not show how the whole (all exports) changed over time. For that purpose, a bar chart like the one in figure 3.5 gives a clearer picture of how the data compare to each other.

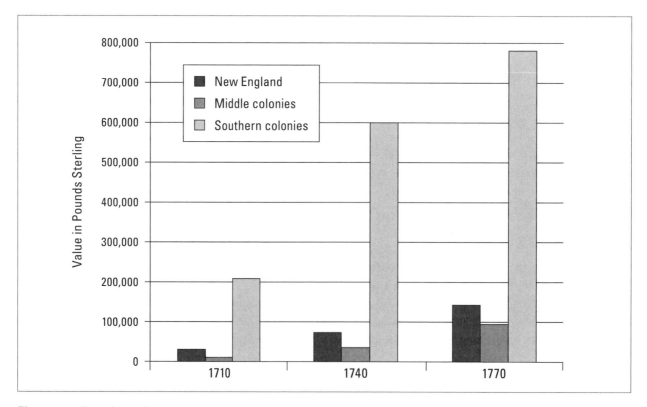

Figure 3.5: Bar chart showing values of colonial exports by region and year.

Source: U.S. Bureau of the Census, 1975.

Graphic texts can be manipulated to emphasize certain characteristics of the data. The bar chart shown in figure 3.5 emphasizes the disparity between values of exports in the southern colonies compared to the other colonies. However, the data shown in figure 3.5 might be rearranged to emphasize growth over time rather than disparity by region, as shown in figure 3.6.

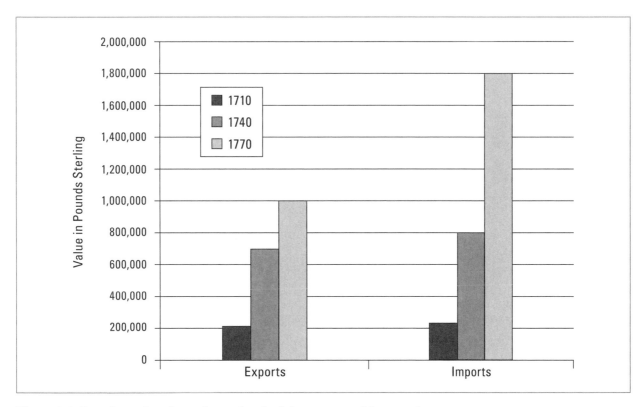

Figure 3.6: Bar chart showing values of colonial exports and imports by year.

Source: U.S. Bureau of the Census, 1975.

Like pie charts, bar charts have certain drawbacks. They are limited as to how many variables they can express. In figure 3.6, the data are expressed in terms of exports and imports, but the variable of region is not included. Figure 3.5 shows regions and exports, but does not include imports. While searching for information about which colonial region had the highest export values during the Revolutionary War period, students may encounter any of the graphic texts in figures 3.4, 3.5, or 3.6. Students should pay attention to what information authors choose to include and exclude from various types of graphic texts. Often these decisions reveal biases and can prompt students to investigate a topic or set of data further.

Another kind of graphic text is a line graph. Like bar graphs, line graphs can represent multiple characteristics of information as quantities rather than percentages. Moreover, line graphs typically represent change over time, as seen in figure 3.7 (page 46).

As shown in figure 3.7, line graphs can display a great deal of information simultaneously. Here, it is easy to see that imports to the southern colonies saw the greatest increase in value from 1710 to 1770. Each of the three types of graphs has strengths and weaknesses depending on the message one wants to convey. It is important that students not only know how to read and interpret each kind of graph but are also aware that the type of chart or graph represents a specific perspective from which an author wants to present information. By recognizing and evaluating the author's perspective, students can make informed choices about the quality and veracity of information they encounter in these visual types of texts.

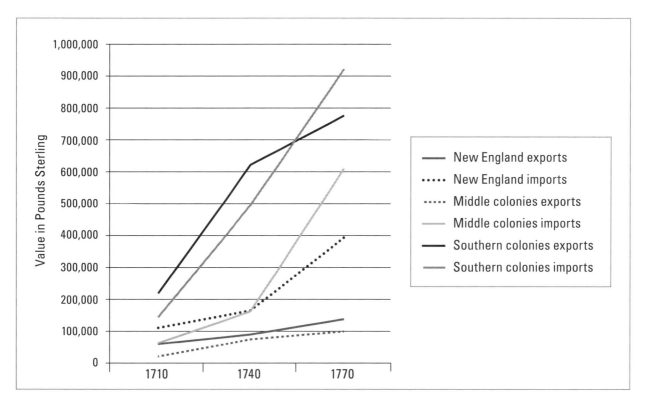

Figure 3.7: Line graph showing values of colonial exports and imports by region and year.

Source: U.S. Bureau of the Census, 1975.

The final type of graphic texts addressed by Mosenthal and Kirsch (1990a, 1990d) are maps. While answering questions about places associated with the American Revolution and colonial America, students might encounter a map on a website depicting the route of Paul Revere's famous ride through the area around Charlestown, Lexington, and Cambridge. Such a map could be particularly helpful to a student trying to answer the question, Where did the events described in Longfellow's poem "Paul Revere's Ride" take place? This map would be an example of a thematic map, which is designed to communicate specific information relative to specific places. Other examples of thematic maps include weather maps (information about climate conditions), topographical maps (information about terrain), or maps that show a phenomenon (for example, information about the spread and incidence of certain diseases).

In contrast to thematic maps, general reference maps show easily recognizable features of a particular area. A general reference map of a town will often include streets, parks, rivers, and highways. A general reference map of North America might show mountain ranges, rivers, lakes, and state or provincial borders. Internet and electronic maps (such as Google Maps) are usually general reference maps by default, but some can be customized by users to turn them into thematic maps (for example, maps that show all the bike trails in an area). Both thematic and general reference maps can be used to identify or clarify the location of specific events, but thematic maps can also be used to make a point about the prevalence or absence of a specific phenomenon. For example, to demonstrate that the earth's climate is steadily growing hotter, an author can use a thematic map showing average temperatures in specific U.S. cities over several years.

We provide the following recommendations for acquainting students with graphic texts.

1. Teach students about the four types of graphic texts, using the previous examples (or others like them). Point out the following important features of graphic texts:

   - Often, graphic texts are used to express information that could also be represented in list form. Graphic texts make information easier to conceptualize or compare.

   - Pie charts, bar charts, and line graphs all present information in terms of a unit of measurement. In pie charts, that unit is limited to a percentage. In bar charts and line graphs, many different units of measure can be used (for example, dollars, years, inches, and so on).

   - Often, graphic texts are created from lists of information (that is, matrix texts). One can understand a graphic text by identifying the list of information it was created from and formulating sentences that summarize the data in a graph. For example, one section of a pie chart showing the percentages of a barrel of crude oil used to produce various products could be read, "46.2 percent of crude oil goes to produce gasoline for automobiles." Like matrix texts, reading graphic texts using a sentence format can help one understand the information more clearly.

   - Understanding matrix texts can help one find locations on a map. Many maps have indexes: lists of locations with letter-number coordinates for each one. The letter-number coordinates correspond to columns and rows on the map. By looking in the appropriate cell formed by a column and row, a location can be found more easily.

2. Ask students to find examples of the different types of graphic texts in print or online sources and bring copies to class.

3. Ask students to sort the graphic texts they found into different types (such as pie charts, bar graphs, line graphs, general reference maps, and thematic maps).

4. Ask questions that prompt students to find and use information in various graphic texts. For example, if a student brought in a line graph showing increases in average daily temperatures in the Rocky Mountains over the past five years, the teacher might ask, "What was the difference in average daily temperature in Leadville between 2009 and 2013?"

5. Ask students to find important features of different kinds of graphic texts (chart labels, measurement scales, scale titles, legends, and so on) and to evaluate the effectiveness of various charts, graphs, and maps.

The following vignette depicts how a teacher can facilitate students' exploration and use of graphic texts to answer questions.

Miss Loftner's students have found a wide variety of charts, graphs, and maps and brought them to class for analysis. Miss Loftner displays a pie chart that Orion found on the board. It has three sections labeled 70 percent, 60 percent, and 63 percent. Each section represents the percentage of the population expected to vote for a certain candidate in the upcoming election.

"They don't add up to 100 percent," someone immediately says.

"Yeah, that's why I brought it," says Orion. "It's really bad. I saw it on the news. Apparently, people in their survey were allowed to pick more than one candidate. I can't believe they chose a pie chart to display the data."

Miss Loftner agrees that a pie chart was not a good choice, and the class discusses which graphic texts would have been better choices. Next, Miss Loftner displays a map that Kevin found. It is an animated map used by an oil company to illustrate the benefits of building an oil pipeline in a certain location. As the animation plays, Kevin narrates.

"Watch this part carefully," he says. "It shows the oil tanker sailing up a wide-open channel to this little town where the pipeline ends. Looks easy, right?"

Kevin then opens a map of the same area on Google Maps.

"Compare this map to the one in the video," he says. "See all those islands in the channel? The oil company left them out of their map to make the passage look easier. It's actually far more complicated and risky to get oil tankers to the end of the pipeline."

Finally, Miss Loftner's class looks at a bar graph that Jenna found.

"I think this is a really good graphic text," she says. "It shows the percentages of saturated, polyunsaturated, and monounsaturated fats in different kinds of oils, like canola, safflower, corn, olive, soybean, peanut, and coconut oil. I like it because each bar is divided into three parts, one for each type of fat. It lets me make a quick decision about which oils are healthiest and helps me explain why I made that decision."

Miss Loftner agrees and asks Jenna what the characteristics of healthy oils are, a category question. After Jenna answers, she follows up with an elaboration question, asking Jenna to explain why healthy oils have high levels of mono- and polyunsaturated fats. Jenna says she'll have to do some more research, and Miss Loftner reminds her to keep track of the sources she finds to use as evidence for her answer.

Mimetic Texts

Mimetic texts are those that mimic real life. That is, they show what objects look like or how items change or are affected by processes and procedures. Mosenthal and Kirsch (1991b, 1991c; Kirsch & Mosenthal, 1990a, 1990b, 1991) reviewed two types of mimetic texts: pictures and schematics. Pictures or simple line drawings are the most basic type of mimetic text. If they are unlabeled, readers must infer which features are important. In response to a question about equipment typically associated with minutemen or American soldiers during the Revolutionary War, students might consult artwork such as Emanuel Leutze's *Washington Crossing the Delaware*, William Barnes Wollen's *The Battle of Lexington*, A. M. Willard's *The Spirit of '76*, John Trumbull's *Battle of Bunker Hill*, or George Willoughby Maynard's *Soldier of the Revolution*, shown in figure 3.8.

A student could infer from the painting in figure 3.8 that American soldiers wore tricorn hats, dark jackets with buttons and collars, and white breeches or riding pants. Students may also notice that this soldier is carrying a rifle and a flag. However, from this picture alone, students couldn't be sure

Figure 3.8: George Willoughby Maynard's *Soldier of the Revolution.*

which of those features were generally true and which were simply true of the soldier in this picture. For making generalizations about a category, picture lists, like the one shown in figure 3.9, are more useful. This is because they allow readers to compare features of several examples of an item and observe commonalities between them. This is similar to the process that students use to answer category questions; they generate a list of examples in a category and draw conclusions about the category based on similarities and differences between the examples. Therefore, a student who was asked, "What are characteristics of Revolutionary War rifles?" could use figure 3.9 to generate a list of features.

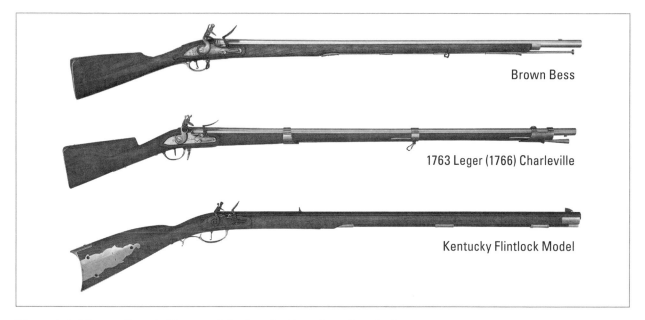

Figure 3.9: Picture list of rifles used during the American Revolution.

Source: Davide Pedersoli & C., 2010a, 2010b, 2010c. Used with permission.

Figure 3.9 shows a picture list of rifles that would have been used by American patriots during the American Revolution. By examining all three, students learn that rifles were generally long, had a smaller metal shaft along the bottom, and were mainly made of wood with metal used for the firing mechanism. While useful, this definition is not as specific as it could be, since it does not use specific names for different parts of the rifle. Figure 3.10 is an example of a labeled picture that students could use to refine the language they use to talk about rifles of the American Revolution.

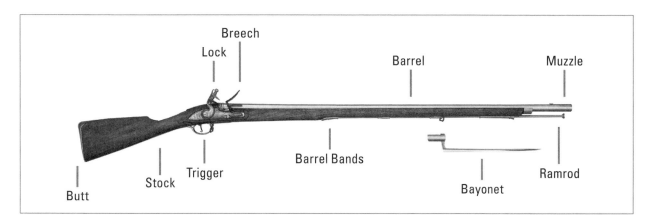

Figure 3.10: Labeled picture of a musket.

Source: Engineer comp geek, 2009.

Using the picture list in figure 3.9 (page 49) and the labeled picture in figure 3.10, students are able to express their observations clearly and explicitly. A student might observe that all three rifles in figure 3.9 have long barrels with ramrods running along the base of the barrel and that the stock was normally made of wood but could be decorated with metal. The student also notes that moving parts of the firing mechanism such as the breech, lock, trigger, and barrel of the gun were made of metal, and that bayonets were detachable pieces that could be attached to the barrel of a gun when necessary. As shown here, pictures are useful for illustrating the important parts and characteristics of an item. That is, they are excellent for illustrating what something is like, but not how it works. For that purpose, schematics are far more effective.

Schematics can convey three major types of information: causes, procedures, and processes. First, a causation schematic shows various causes of an event or phenomenon. Students could consult a causation schematic like the one in figure 3.11 to answer the question, What effect did mercantilism have on the Revolutionary War?

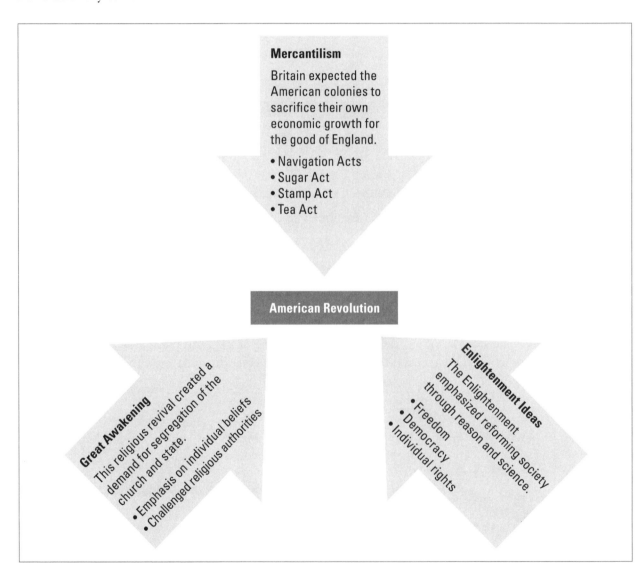

Figure 3.11: Causation schematic for the American Revolution.

The schematic in figure 3.11 shows various causes for the American Revolution. Often, authors use causation schematics when they want to communicate that an effect may have multiple causes. Students should be aware that causation schematics may not show *all* of the causes for something, but rather may show those the author wants to emphasize. Additionally, causation schematics typically give equal weight to each cause they feature. For example, figure 3.11 seems to indicate that mercantilism, the Great Awakening, and Enlightenment ideas were equally responsible for the American Revolution, which is not necessarily the case. Students should be aware of the biases that may be present in schematics of this type and evaluate them carefully to detect misleading information.

The second type of schematic, a procedural schematic, shows how things move or function or how to do something. When looking for an answer to the question, What was the effect of the printing press on the Revolutionary War? students might encounter a procedural schematic like the one in figure 3.12. The schematic in figure 3.12 might prompt students to infer that printing presses allowed information to be reproduced more efficiently, allowing for wider distribution of ideas, which in turn fueled revolutionary thinking.

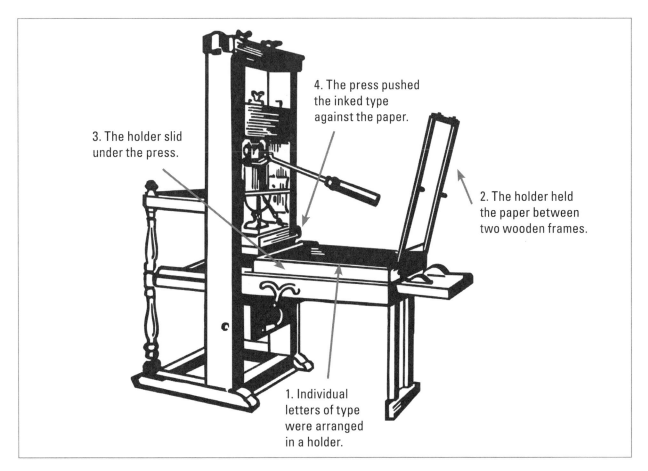

4. The press pushed the inked type against the paper.

3. The holder slid under the press.

2. The holder held the paper between two wooden frames.

1. Individual letters of type were arranged in a holder.

Figure 3.12: Procedural schematic for a colonial printing press.

Figure 3.12 fulfills a double purpose. Like a labeled picture, it gives students information about what the various parts of the printing press are called. However, using arrows and descriptive sentences, it also explains how one would go about using the printing press to print a newspaper or other document. The overlapping nature of various texts illustrated by this procedural schematic is an important feature of all texts. Often, two texts will give the same information, but one will give a better or more complete version of the information. Students should be aware of how much information a text conveys and select the most useful texts to study.

The final type of mimetic text is a process schematic. Process schematics show how something changes over time. Pictures in science textbooks of the stages of metamorphosis or the stages of plant growth from seed to tree are excellent examples of process schematics. A student seeking evidence for her conclusion that Boston was an important city that grew rapidly during the post-Revolutionary War period might use the process schematic in figure 3.13 to support her claim.

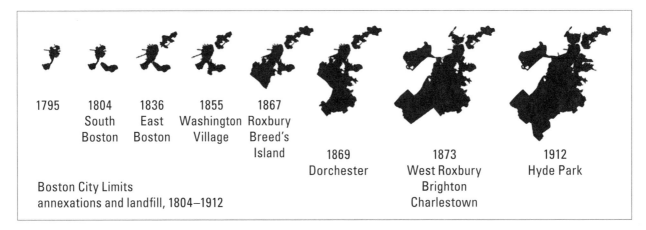

Figure 3.13: Process schematic showing the growth of Boston from 1795–1912.

Source: Rankin (Yale University), 2005, www.radicalcartography.net. Used with permission.

The process schematic in figure 3.13 not only shows how Boston grew and changed over time but also allows students to compare each of the stages. For example, students could examine figure 3.13 to conclude that Boston grew to almost ten times its original size between 1795 and 1912. Students could compare this process schematic to ones showing other cities' growth.

We provide the following recommendations for acquainting students with mimetic texts.

1. Teach students about the three types of mimetic texts, using the previous examples (or others like them). Point out the following important features of mimetic texts:

    *   Picture texts might be individual pictures, picture lists, or labeled pictures. Looking at a picture is similar to answering category questions: one is trying to figure out which characteristics are common to a category (such as military clothes or rifles).

    *   Procedural and process schematics show changes over time.

    *   Like other nonlinguistic texts, mimetic texts often overlap with the other types of texts. For example, a procedural schematic might include pictures and labels in addition to showing a procedure.

2. Ask students to find examples of the different types of mimetic texts in print or online sources and bring copies to class.

3. Ask students to sort the mimetic texts they found into different types (such as pictures, picture lists, labeled pictures, procedural schematics, and process schematics).

4. Ask questions that prompt students to make generalizations about categories based on mimetic texts. For example, if a student brought in a picture list of various types of brass instruments, the teacher might ask, "What is common to all brass instruments?"

The following vignette depicts how a teacher can help facilitate students' exploration and use of mimetic texts to answer questions.

> Mr. Phin's science class has been studying nuclear reactors, and while students understand that nuclear reactors use nuclear fission to produce energy, many are still unable to answer elaboration questions about where the energy comes from and how it gets turned into electricity. To help them understand, and to explain the features of mimetic texts, Mr. Phin uses a procedural schematic.
>
> "In this case, a procedural schematic is best because of the labels and arrows," he explains. "The labels show you what is happening at each stage of the process," he says as he walks students through each stage, explaining how the control bars are lowered toward the reactor core to split uranium atoms, which produces heat. "This arrow indicates that the heated water moves through the steam generator, which turns the turbines," he continues.
>
> Mr. Phin reviews the rest of the process with students. Then, he asks students to answer an elaboration prompt: Using the procedural schematic, explain why nuclear fission is an effective way to produce energy. He then asks students to use the same schematic to list the effects of various broken parts on a nuclear reactor and to explain what would happen if, for example, the water circulation pump broke. The class discusses further how the procedural schematic helped them to visualize the inner workings of a power plant and how other mimetic texts could have been used.

Electronic Texts

As the Internet and technology are used more and more in schools, students will frequently encounter texts electronically on a screen. Students can apply what they know about linguistic and nonlinguistic text structures to help them understand electronic texts: if a text consists mainly of words arranged into paragraphs, they look for the five linguistic text structures; if a text is mainly composed of images or graphics, they look for the three nonlinguistic text structures. However, reading text on a screen is fundamentally different from reading text in books, magazines, and other printed sources. Here, we describe how teachers can help students effectively interact with texts they encounter on computer screens, on tablets and e-readers, and on their smartphones and other mobile devices.

Reading electronic text is different from reading printed text for two reasons. First, electronic texts do not normally stay still. Often, users scroll through the text or resize the window to better fit the text. Unlike the page of a book, text read on smartphones, tablets, laptops, or e-readers may appear at the top, bottom, side, or center of the screen depending on how the device is oriented or where the reader began reading. Second, electronic texts are distinguished from traditional texts by the inclusion of hyperlinks and search features. These allow students to quickly link from one text to another and search for a myriad of texts on a certain topic.

Christopher Sanchez and Jennifer Wiley (2009) reported that scrolling text was harder to comprehend and remember than printed text. They explained, "Nonscrolling interfaces produced significantly better comprehension overall than did scrolling interfaces. . . . Whereas scrolling did lead to worse performance overall, there was a more pronounced effect for those individuals who had lower WMC [working memory capacity]" (p. 734). Scrolling text also prevented students from developing a deep understanding of the causes and effects in a text. In 2011, Sanchez and Russell Branaghan investigated how reading text on small devices (like smartphones or tablets) affected one's recall and reasoning. They concluded,

> Small displays produced lower overall reasoning performance, and also increased the amount of time it took to solve the problems relative to a full-size display. This suggests that while factual information gathering is unaffected when done [sic] a small device, reasoning performance is negatively affected when done on a small device. (p. 796)

These results indicate that reading scrolling text or text on a small screen may have negative effects on students' comprehension and reasoning abilities. To counteract these effects, teachers can encourage students to read Internet texts on desktop computers or laptops. They might also suggest that once students have found a text worth reading, they print it out and read it from the printed pages.

Second, reading online text requires more comprehension skills than reading printed text. Jane David (2009) observed that "reading online demands different skills than reading print-only texts does" (p. 84). She summarized research that found that "reading for understanding online requires the same skills as offline reading, including using prior knowledge and making predictions, *plus* a set of additional critical-thinking skills that reflect the open-ended, continually changing online context" (pp. 84–85). Julie Coiro (2005) observed that Internet texts "demand higher levels of inferential reasoning and comprehension monitoring strategies that help readers stay on task" (p. 30). The problems of Internet reading are often compounded for less skilled readers because they are "unsure where to focus their attention and unable to call on alternative strategies if they don't find what they are searching for" (Coiro, 2005, p. 30). Therefore, it is crucial that teachers prepare all students to read Internet texts.

Nicholas Burbules and Thomas Callister (2000) emphasized the importance of students having a specific goal when reading on the Internet. Els Kuiper, Monique Volman, and Jan Terwel (2005) stated that students must learn "to ask themselves continually what it is they want to know, what is the purpose of knowing it, and what sort of information can contribute to that purpose" (p. 305). To accomplish this, we recommend teaching students to read Internet texts in small chunks, stopping after each paragraph or section of text to ask themselves three questions:

1. What do I want to know?

2. Did what I just read tell me anything about that?

3. Do I think the next section of text will tell me something about that?

If students answer no to the second or third question, they should skim the rest of the text to find a section they think *will* be helpful or find a different text to read. The following vignette depicts how a teacher can help facilitate students' use of electronic texts to answer questions.

Mrs. Hill's students consider themselves to be experts with technology, but Mrs. Hill recognizes that being able to use electronic devices doesn't guarantee that students have the skills to effectively obtain information from electronic texts. So she gives her students a process to use when looking for and reading information on the Internet.

"First, be clear about what you want to know," she says. "If you're trying to find information to answer the question, What are examples of governments that have gone bankrupt? you might use keywords such as *government* and *bankrupt.*"

She then discusses other ways that students can narrow their searches by using keywords and Boolean operators before discussing strategies for staying on task while reading. She says, "As you read, always ask yourself whether the paragraph you just read told you anything new about your topic. If it didn't, you may want to look elsewhere."

Mrs. Hill explains that before they start to read in depth, they should try to find two or three texts that relate directly to the question they're trying to answer and are credible.

Finally, she reviews the research on scrolling and electronic texts with her students and cautions them, saying, "Reading text on an electronic device can keep you from understanding it as well as printed text. So, once you find two or three good texts, print them out and read from the printouts, if you can. If not, give yourself extra time to read the text on screen. Try to eliminate distractions so that you can focus all your attention on what the text is saying."

Mrs. Hill engages her students in several activities to help them become comfortable with the process, including one in which they compare their comprehension of electronic text to their comprehension of printed text and another in which they evaluate search results that show up in online searches.

Information From Multiple Texts

In addition to understanding what to expect from the structures and information found in various types of texts, students should understand how to collect and synthesize information from multiple sources and different types of texts. Wiley and her colleagues (2009) observed,

> The collection of information across multiple sources is a characteristic of authentic research in many disciplines. . . . Historians use multiple sources to corroborate accounts. In literary studies, analysts draw on close readings of multiple bits of information within and across texts. (p. 1095)

Here, we offer suggestions for how teachers can train students to look for and synthesize information from multiple sources.

As explained previously, gathering information from multiple texts, both printed and online, and synthesizing that information into meaningful generalizations and conclusions will enable students to answer teachers' questions when they do not already possess the requisite background knowledge. First of all, students should have a clear idea of what information they are looking for. If they are at the detail phase of the questioning sequence, they might be seeking information to answer questions like, What places are associated with George Washington? If they are at the category phase of the questioning sequence, they might be looking for information about the characteristics of various American presidents. If they are at the elaboration phase of the questioning sequence, they might be seeking information that explains why American presidents must be thirty-five or older. If they are at the evidence phase of the questioning sequence, they might be looking for different perspectives on their assertions. Whatever phase they are at in the questioning sequence, students should always be able to describe the information they are seeking in detail.

Once students have described what they are looking for, they should identify what they already know and what they don't know. For example, a student answering a category question such as, What are other examples of U.S. presidents besides George Washington? might be able to list several American presidents but knows that she needs to find even more names. Kirsch and Mosenthal (1992) suggested that a "known/need-to-know" strategy be used to locate specific information:

1. Figure out what you already know that will help you answer the question.

2. Figure out what information you need to find to be able to answer the question.

3. Search for texts that contain information that matches what you already know (this helps you confirm that what you already know is true).

4. Look for the information you need to find near the information you already know.

Sometimes, students will need to look for information in cycles. For example, a student examining a nested list to answer a detail question discovers that the southern colonies imported £920,248 worth of goods in 1770. This prompts him to look for additional information, such as which colonies were considered southern colonies and why their imports were so much higher than the other colonies. Therefore, the student returns to step 1 of the known/need-to-know sequence to look for information related to the new questions. Students can use an organizer like the one in figure 3.14 to keep track of what information they are looking for, what they already know, what they need to know, and what further information they need to find in the future. The known/need-to-know strategy can be used during any phase of the questioning sequence in which students need to seek information. During the elaboration phase, a student may need additional information to answer a question such as, What effect did the available weaponry have on the outcome of the Revolutionary War? During the evidence phase, a student might need to seek additional information to provide adequate support for his elaborations.

Question I'm trying to answer: _____

What I already know: _____

What I need to know: _____

Information that I've already found: _____

Information that I still need to find: _____

Figure 3.14: Known/need-to-know organizer.

Visit **marzanoresearch.com/classroomstrategies** for a reproducible version of this figure.

Once students have found all the information they need, they combine—or synthesize—that information to answer their original question. This is an excellent opportunity for students to use what they have learned about different texts to select and fill in a specific textual structure to synthesize the information they have found. For example, a student uses a causation structure to explain why American presidents must be thirty-five or older; a student who has found names of American presidents uses a simple list to compile their names or a compound list to compile their names in addition to information about their presidencies (such as years in office, political party, and major accomplishments); a student who has found information about places associated with George Washington creates a map that shows the locations of important battles that he won; or a student who has found information about the causes of Britain's surrender to the American patriots uses a causation schematic to synthesize his findings.

Summary

Students get information from two places to answer questions: their prior knowledge and external sources. In this chapter, we reviewed three major text types that students will need to be familiar with to find information during questioning sequences. Linguistic texts usually follow one of five structures: (1) description, (2) sequence, (3) causation, (4) problem/solution, or (5) comparison. The three types of nonlinguistic texts—(1) matrix, (2) graphic, and (3) mimetic texts—also follow predictable structures. These structures help students know what to expect and look for as they gather information from print and electronic sources. When reading electronic sources, students can use specific strategies to improve their comprehension of electronic texts and can employ a known/need-to-know strategy to help find and synthesize information from multiple sources.

Chapter 3: Comprehension Questions

1. Why is it important for students to be familiar with different linguistic and nonlinguistic text types and structures?

2. Describe the five linguistic text structures reviewed in this chapter and explain how students can identify them.

3. How can teachers help students practice identifying and interpreting nonlinguistic texts?

4. How are electronic texts similar to and different from linguistic and nonlinguistic texts?

5. How can teachers help students find and synthesize information from multiple texts?

Chapter 4

RESPONSE STRATEGIES

Every question a teacher asks is designed to elicit a response from students. The process by which students respond should not be left up to chance or expediency. Rather, teachers should provide structured activities that maximize the usefulness of students' responses. Teachers can think of response strategies as falling into two categories: (1) strategies to be used when students respond individually and (2) strategies to be used when students respond in groups. Additionally, teachers can use specific strategies to help facilitate productive collaborative work among students.

Individual Student Responses

Individual students often respond to questions that are posed during whole-group discussions or activities. Specific response strategies can allow teachers to call on multiple students for each question, give students the chance to rehearse their responses before being called on, ask students to defend their responses, call on students randomly, ask students to record their responses, or allow students to challenge each other's responses. Strategies for individual student responses include chaining and voting, paired response, peer instruction, random names, short written responses, and accuracy checks.

Response Chaining and Voting

Response chaining and voting both allow the teacher to call on multiple students to answer each question asked. This allows individual student responses to be strung together to create a class discussion rather than a simple back-and-forth between the teacher and one student. The goal of response chaining is to identify correct information by having students respond to each other's answers. Response chaining involves four steps:

1. The teacher poses a question.

2. Student A responds to the question.

3. The teacher asks student B to identify student A's answer as correct, incorrect, or partially correct and explain why.

4. If student B incorrectly identifies student A's answer, the teacher can call on student C to respond to student B's response.

For example, in response to a detail question about a cause-and-effect relationship found in a text, a particular student identifies one cause for a specific event. When the teacher calls on another student to respond, that student identifies the first student's answer as partially correct, explaining that the event had several causes. The teacher calls on a third student to ask if she agrees that there were several causes and to ask her to list the unidentified causes.

Alternatively, the teacher could have the entire class vote on the accuracy of student A's response, identify the correct response after the class votes, and call on student B to explain why the correct answer is correct. Additionally, if student A's answer was correct and student B identifies it as correct, the teacher could ask student B to add additional information to student A's answer. To add physical movement to this strategy, a teacher uses a small foam ball to signal which student is responsible for responding. The teacher throws the ball to student A, who passes it to student B when he or she is selected to respond, who then passes it to student C, and so on. The following vignette illustrates a teacher using response chaining during a mathematics lesson.

> Jamison has just answered a category question by explaining that the difference between a permutation and a combination is that in a permutation, the order of the items matters.
>
> "A permutation is an ordered combination," says Jamison.
>
> The teacher then asks Anetta what she thinks about Jamison's answer.
>
> "I think he's right," she says.
>
> When the teacher prompts her to expand on Jamison's answer, Anetta gives an example, saying, "If I was making fruit salad with apples, grapes, and melon, order wouldn't matter. There would be four different combinations no matter what order I listed the fruits in: apples and grapes, apples and melon, grapes and melon, or all three. Those would be combinations. But if I was designing a combination lock and wanted to figure out how many different combinations I could make using 1, 2, and 3, order would matter: there are six different permutations of those numbers. The lock should really be called a permutation lock!"
>
> The teacher thanks Anetta for her answer and asks Carlos to comment on Anetta's response. After Carlos responds, the teacher corrects any misconceptions and then asks another question.

Paired Response

Paired response has several distinct advantages. First, it gets all students involved in answering every question. Second, it prompts less confident students to try to answer each question. Finally, it allows students to benefit from their peers' knowledge. To use paired response, the teacher organizes students into pairs before asking any questions. When a question is asked, pairs confer and decide on their answer to the question. Then, the teacher calls on a pair. One member of the pair can verbalize the pair's answer, or both partners can contribute. For example, in a science class, the teacher asks students a detail question about how to solve an equation involving circular motion. One student in the pair might be excellent at math and therefore better able to perform the necessary calculations. The other student in the pair might be better at conceptualizing the problem and explaining what the end result of the calculations means. When the teacher asks that pair to respond, the first student explains her calculations while the second student explains what the answer means and how it addresses the original question. The following vignette illustrates this strategy being used during a social studies lesson.

Ms. Pillar has asked her students the detail question, What does the term hemisphere mean?

Betti and Marissa are partners for that day, so Betti turns to Marissa and says, "It's half of the earth. Like the northern hemisphere and the southern hemisphere. The equator is the dividing line."

Marissa thinks and then says, "Yeah, but there are eastern and western hemispheres too. There's a line that goes through England that divides them. I think it's called the prime meridian."

When the teacher calls on them, Betti explains that the equator divides the northern hemisphere from the southern, and Marissa explains that the prime meridian divides the eastern and western hemispheres.

Ms. Pillar probes a little deeper with a follow-up question, asking, "Does the prime meridian go all the way around the world, or is there another imaginary line on the opposite side of the earth from it?"

Students confer with their partners again before Ms. Pillar calls on a different pair to share their answer.

Peer Instruction

In some cases, teachers may want to structure detail questions as multiple choice so that students can select the best answer from a list of potential answers. For example, to ask an elaboration question in a multiple-choice format, a teacher might list several causes or consequences associated with an event and ask students to identify the one they think is most important. Or a teacher might ask students to identify the most important belief associated with a certain organization or group from a list of popular beliefs from that time period. Peer instruction is a technique well-suited to these types of questions.

In 1997, Eric Mazur described the process for peer instruction as follows:

1. Pose a question.

2. Give students time to think about it.

3. Collect initial student responses from the entire class and let students know which answers were chosen most often, but don't reveal the correct answer.

4. Ask each student to defend his or her answer by convincing his or her neighbors that it is correct.

5. Collect revised student responses from the entire class and discuss the new distribution of responses.

6. Explain the correct answer.

Mazur found many benefits to this form of questioning. Because students have to explain their answers to their neighbors, "students do not merely assimilate the material presented to them; they must think for themselves and put their thoughts into words" (p. 14). Mazur also found that peer instruction resulted in better student understanding of underlying concepts (rather than isolated facts or processes) and increased student engagement and satisfaction with learning experiences.

An important part of peer instruction is collecting student responses from the entire class and letting students know which responses were most common. Teachers can use many techniques to accomplish this, such as show of hands, hand signals (1 finger = choice A, 2 fingers = choice B, and so on), or response cards (students write their answers on small papers or whiteboards and display them simultaneously). However, student response technologies, or "clickers," offer a host of benefits that make them an ideal match for peer instruction. These remote-control-like devices allow students to submit their individual answers to questions electronically. The teacher can then view individual student responses on a computer or project a graph of student responses for the entire class to see. Regarding clickers, Jeffrey Stowell and Jason Nelson (2007) found that

> the most apparent advantage of using the clickers was the increased honesty of student feedback. . . . The clicker group's answers during the lecture more closely reflected how much they were actually learning, whereas those in the hand-raising group appeared to be influenced by social conformity. . . . Use of response cards, which are more anonymous than hand-raising but less anonymous than the clickers, also appears to be susceptible to social influence. (pp. 256–257)

Additionally, the software associated with most student response systems tallies and visually displays student answers, allowing the teacher to quickly display the class's initial and revised patterns of responses. Ian Beatty and William Gerace (2009) explained that the

> chart showing the distribution of students' answers also adds value to the process. It is not just a way to find out how many picked which answer; as Roschelle et al. (2004a) note, it is also a "high contrast display that drive[s] productive discourse" (p. 28). It makes differences in students' positions starkly obvious. One glance strongly conveys whether the class is in agreement (a single peak), generally undecided (a uniform or random spread), or highly polarized (two distinct peaks). (p. 158)

The following vignette illustrates how a language arts teacher can use peer instruction and student response technologies to ask questions during the detail phase of a questioning sequence.

> Mrs. Cullingford's class is studying *The Canterbury Tales*. Mrs. Cullingford displays the following text, along with a question, and asks students to respond using their clickers.
>
> Description of the Prioress from Chaucer's *Canterbury Tales*:
>
> > But for to speken of her conscience
> > She was so charitable and so pitous
> > She woulde weep if that she saw a mouse
> > Caught in a trap, if it were dead or bled.
> > Of smalle houndes had she that she fed
> > With roasted flesh or milk or wastel bread,
> > But sore wept she if one of them were dead
> > Or if men smote it with a yarde, smart;
> > And all was conscience and tender heart.
>
> Do you think Chaucer's portrait of the Prioress's "conscience" and charity is meant to make us:
>
> A. Sympathetic toward her love of animals?
> B. Critical of her misplaced priorities?
> C. Aware that women are more tender-hearted than men?
>
> *Question source: Elizabeth Cullingford, English, University of Texas at Austin (as cited in Bruff, 2009, p. 87).*
>
> Students respond, and Mrs. Cullingford displays the following pattern of responses:

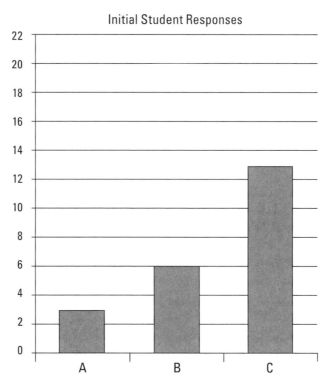

Mrs. Cullingford then asks students to discuss their answers, with each student explaining why he or she thinks his or her answer is correct. The buzz of talk fills the room for several minutes. Then, Mrs. Cullingford asks students to vote again and displays the distribution of students' revised answers.

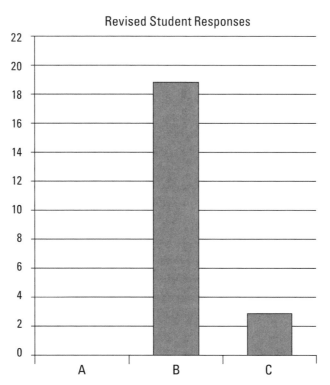

Mrs. Cullingford points out that most students have selected B and asks several students who changed their answer to B to explain why they changed.

Random Names

The random names strategy can be used to keep all students engaged in answering questions during the detail phase of a questioning sequence. For this strategy, the teacher writes each student's name on a separate slip of paper or popsicle stick and places all the names in a jar, bowl, or hat. After asking a question, the teacher selects a student's name at random to give an answer. The teacher continues to select names until he or she feels that enough answers have been submitted. Then she adds all students' names back into the jar (even if all students' names have not yet been called) before asking a new question. This encourages students to pay attention to every question, since there is always a chance that their name will be chosen.

The teacher could use random names in tandem with response chaining strategies to have subsequent students respond to an initial answer. For example, a teacher asks students detail questions about natural phenomena that affected the outcome of the American Revolution such as Washington's winter at Valley Forge or the Great Hurricane of 1780. First, the teacher asks students about the place, time period, and events associated with Washington's winter at Valley Forge. Drawing names out of the jar, the teacher asks each student to explain one detail about the phenomena. When a satisfactory number of answers have been given, the teacher restores the selected names to the jar and asks her next series of questions about the Great Hurricane of 1780. The following vignette illustrates this strategy.

> Mrs. Rogers is asking her class detail questions about Washington's winter at Valley Forge. She selects a name from her random names jar.
>
> "Sal," she reads, smiling. "What dangers were associated with Washington's winter at Valley Forge?"
>
> Sal thinks for a moment and then says, "A lot of soldiers died, and a lot of equipment was ruined from the wet and the cold."
>
> Mrs. Rogers thanks Sal and selects another name: Jefry.
>
> "What advantages were associated with Washington's winter at Valley Forge?" Mrs. Rogers asks.
>
> Jefry says, "Valley Forge was a good position for Washington to spend the winter even though it was cold. He protected the members of Congress who were in York, and he kept an eye on the British who were occupying Philadelphia."
>
> After thanking Jefry, Mrs. Rogers selects three more names to answer questions and then returns all five names to the jar before beginning to ask detail questions about the Great Hurricane of 1780.

Short Written Responses

One simple technique for individual student responses is to have students record their answers. This can occur in a number of forms. Academic notebooks provide a very flexible form. With these, students record their individual responses to questions in a notebook dedicated to a specific subject area. Throughout a lesson, students periodically compare their responses to specific questions. It is very useful if student entries are dated so that students can examine the progression of their learning as evidenced by the changes in their entries. For example, on Friday of a given week, students might review their previous entries and make additions or changes to their comments as needed.

An alternative to writing entries in an academic notebook is to record short written responses on pieces of paper that students hand in at the end of class so that the teacher can review them. However, the disadvantage to this approach is that students cannot go back and examine previous responses. The following vignette depicts a teacher using short written responses.

> Mr. Rainne's students are studying ways the geosphere, biosphere, hydrosphere, and atmosphere interact. Mr. Rainne is about to ask a series of category questions, and instructs students to create a table in their academic notebooks. Across the top are the four categories: (1) geosphere, (2) biosphere, (3) hydrosphere, and (4) atmosphere. Each row represents a different category question.
>
> Mr. Rainne begins with example questions. Students write down examples of materials normally found in each Earth system. When students are finished, Mr. Rainne asks them to stand up with their notebooks, find a partner, and compare answers.
>
> "For each person you talk to, try to give them one example they don't have, and get one example from them that you don't have," he instructs.
>
> Students meet with several partners before returning to their desks, where Mr. Rainne continues the questioning sequence by asking them to look at the examples they've written down and list characteristics that the examples have in common. Students write their individual answers, confer with partners, and return to their desks before Mr. Rainne asks specific prompt questions to help students generate additional characteristics.

Accuracy Checks

At any point in time, a teacher or student can call for accuracy checks regarding information offered by other students or the teacher. Of course, this strategy typically requires immediate access to external information, usually found on the Internet. For example, in response to a detail question, one or more students offer information as a matter of fact. The teacher or another student requests that the accuracy of the information be checked, and all students are invited to use the Internet to examine the accuracy of the proposed information. The following vignette illustrates this strategy.

> Mr. Mizuno's school has several sets of digital tablets that teachers can check out and use with their classes. Mr. Mizuno often checks out a set of tablets when he is planning to ask detail questions, especially when he knows that answering those questions may require the use of external sources. He's also taught his students to use Check It! as their peers respond to questions. If any student suspects that the answer given by a peer or information presented by the teacher is inaccurate, or if a student simply wants clarification about information offered, the student can call out, "Check it!" Mr. Mizuno quickly clarifies what information needs to be checked, and then students race to find information on the Internet (using their tablets) that verifies or invalidates the answer given. This works particularly well when a student gives a partially correct answer or an answer that contains an error in reasoning.
>
> During one questioning sequence, Mr. Mizuno asks about Christopher Columbus's preparations for his first voyage, and Beckah says, "It was difficult for him to raise support because most people in Europe thought the world was flat."
>
> Whitnie looks confused for a moment, then raises her hand and calls out, "Check it!" Mr. Mizuno asks students to look for information about 13th century perceptions of the shape of Earth.

Charlie raises his hand after a few minutes of searching and says, "I just read a source that says Eratosthenes measured the circumference of the earth in 240 BC. So he thought it was round."

Other students contribute their findings, and it emerges that although some people in the 13th century believed the world was flat, the educated classes mostly agreed with Greek ideas of the Earth being spherical. In response, Mr. Mizuno points out that Beckah was correct about it being difficult for Columbus to raise support and asks students why it was difficult, if many people already believed the world was round.

Group Responses

Group responses are particularly valuable during the category, elaboration, and evidence phases when questions may involve different perspectives or competing opinions. However, students may interact in groups to answer questions during any phase. There are several strategies that students can use to collaborate in groups and respond collectively, such as sticky-note brainstorming, group listing, paired comparisons, numbered heads together, and quiz-quiz-trade.

Sticky-Note Brainstorming

One strategy that teachers can use for group responses is sticky-note brainstorming. During this strategy, each student receives a marker and a small pad of sticky notes. Then, the teacher poses a question. After the class has answered detail questions about Lee Harvey Oswald, for example, the teacher asks a category question: What are other examples that fit into the category of assassins? Students then write down every example of an assassin they can think of, with each example on a separate sticky note. The name of anyone who might possibly be termed an assassin is a legitimate answer to write on a sticky note. One student writes the following examples, each on a separate sticky note:

- John Wilkes Booth

- The person who killed Archduke Francis Ferdinand

- Nathuram Godse

- Brutus

- Jack the Ripper

- James Bond

- Jason Bourne

As seen here, each student recalls every example he can think of, regardless of whether he knows the person's name (as in the second item), whether he is completely sure that person qualifies as an assassin (for example, James Bond), or whether the person is fictional (for example, Jason Bourne). Once students finish writing, the teacher asks them to stick their sticky notes on the board so that they are visible to the entire class. The class then fills in missing information and discusses which examples might not be defensible as examples of that category. The following vignette illustrates a teacher leading that discussion.

Ms. Volke's class has just brainstormed examples of assassins and affixed their sticky notes to the board. Now that everyone can see the examples, Ms. Volke asks if anyone notices information that needs to be filled in or information that shouldn't actually be included in the category of assassins.

"I know the name of the man who assassinated the Archduke," says Presa. "It was Gavrilo Princip."

Ms. Volke adds this information to the appropriate sticky note and calls on another student, Marco.

"I don't know who Godse is," he says, and Ms. Volke asks Ernesto, who contributed that example, to explain.

Ernesto says that Godse assassinated Mahatma Gandhi.

Finally, Trisha says, "I don't think Jack the Ripper counts as an assassin. I think an assassin kills someone for political or religious reasons. Jack the Ripper was just a murderer."

Based on her comments, the class decides to remove Jack the Ripper and several other examples who are better described as murderers than assassins. Following the class's discussion, Ms. Volke compiles the list of examples and posts it in the room where students can refer to it.

Group Listing

Group listing is another strategy that teachers can use for group responses. For example, a teacher asks the following questions during the category phase of a questioning sequence:

- How are documents that define people's rights and form of government normally written?

- Why are documents that define people's rights and form of government important?

- Who normally writes documents that define people's rights and form of government?

Because there are three questions, the teacher divides the class into three groups. Each group receives a piece of paper with one of the questions written at the top. The group then writes down as many answers to its question as the students can think of. After a predetermined amount of time, the groups rotate lists. Each group receives a page with a new question at the top and the previous groups' ideas listed beneath it. The group adds its ideas, and the lists rotate again. When each group receives back its original list, the teacher asks the groups to organize the lists with the most important characteristics at the top and the less important characteristics at the bottom. The following vignette illustrates a group using this strategy.

Mr. Hucksley's students have been studying documents that define a group of people's rights and form of government such as the Magna Carta, the Declaration of Independence, and the Mayflower Compact. Before asking them to answer category questions, he divides his students into three groups. Martinez's group has the question, How are documents that define people's rights and form of government normally written?

Jakie says, "Well, they're usually drafted by a group of people, not just one person," and Martinez writes that down.

Kile says, "They're usually pretty philosophical too, so there must be some research involved in the process," and Martinez records that answer too.

After several minutes of recording answers, Mr. Hucksley asks the groups to rotate questions, and Martinez's group considers a new question, Why are documents that define people's rights and form of government important? After rotating two more times, Martinez's group receives their original question back, with other groups' answers written beneath their own. They decide that being drafted by a group of people is an important characteristic of this type of document, so they put that characteristic near the top of their final list. Research as a characteristic of the process is placed toward the middle, indicating that it is semi-important. After the group orders all of the characteristics, the students share their final list with the class and explain why they ordered the items as they did.

Paired Comparisons

This strategy is similar to two strategies from *Kagan Cooperative Learning* (Kagan & Kagan, 2009): mix-pair-share and pairs compare. Paired comparisons allow students to answer questions as a group and collaborate about their responses, and they also incorporate movement into a questioning sequence. To use this strategy, the teacher first asks students to stand up and move to a different location in the room. This moves students away from the peers they normally collaborate with while sitting at their desks. Then, the teacher calls out "pair," and students pair up with the person closest to them. Next, she asks a question, and each pair shares their individual answers with each other, discussing any areas of disagreement. The teacher calls out "pairs compare," and each pair of students groups together with another pair to form a group of four. Each pair shares its answer, and the group discusses any areas of disagreement. Finally, she calls on various groups of four and asks them to share their answer, addressing areas of disagreement between groups or misconceptions. The following vignette illustrates this strategy.

Ms. Reale's students have been studying natural phenomena related to the sun, including the aurora borealis and aurora australis. Students listed "appear in different colors" as a characteristic of both the aurora borealis and aurora australis, and during the elaboration phase, Ms. Reale wants them to explain why. After asking students to get up and move to a different area of the room, Ms. Reale calls out, "Pair!"

Lexi and Levon pair up, and Lexi says, "I'm pretty sure it has to do with the chemistry of the air. Do you remember the chart in the textbook that had nitrogen for darker colors like purple and blue and oxygen for lighter colors like green and red?"

"Yeah," says Levon, "but didn't it have to do with the altitude too? Like, higher up was green and blue and lower down was red and purple?"

Lexi and Levon settle on their answer, and Ms. Reale calls out, "Pairs compare!" Lexi and Levon pair up with Jason and Tony. When they compare answers, Jason and Tony point out that they agree about the nitrogen and oxygen but that Lexi and Levon have the altitudes backwards. They show Lexi and Levon a chart they drew. The four also refine their answer to specify that the auroras happen when atoms of different particles collide in the earth's atmosphere. When Ms. Reale calls on the group, Jason shares their answer and the chart they made.

Numbered Heads Together

This strategy was also designed by Spencer Kagan and Miguel Kagan (2009). Here, the teacher asks students to form small groups and number off in each group. So, if students form groups of four, each person in the group is assigned a number from 1 to 4. If groups have five members, students number off 1 to 5, and so on. Then, the teacher asks a question. For example, an English teacher asks an elaboration question: Why are connotative meanings of words important when speaking to specific audiences? Within their groups, students compare answers. The goal is for everyone in the group to have an answer ready. After groups have time to confer, the teacher calls for their attention and announces a number. The student in each group who has that number stands, and the teacher asks one or more of the standing students to answer the question. The teacher helps resolve any misconceptions or areas of disagreement before students sit down, and the process is repeated for the next question. The following vignette illustrates this strategy.

> Mr. Petrites's students have been studying the use of rhetoric in the context of public speaking. Before asking elaboration questions, Mr. Petrites asks students to form groups of three and number off.
>
> After students have their numbers, Mr. Petrites asks, "Why are connotative meanings of words important when speaking to specific audiences?"
>
> Carlisle, Amie, and Jack are in a group together. Jack shrugs his shoulders, but Amie says, "Different audiences have different points of view. If you're speaking to a group of moms, you'll want to use words that have different connotations than if you're speaking to a group of businesspeople. Their values are different."
>
> Carlisle listens and then asks, "But I thought connotative meaning was like the definition of a word. So what you said doesn't make sense."
>
> Amie responds, "No, connotative meaning is like a charged meaning. Like if I said 'illegal alien' instead of 'undocumented worker.' Connotations usually carry positive or negative feelings or meanings."
>
> Jack says, "Oh, I get it! Like the difference between *confident* and *arrogant*. They both refer to attitudes, but one means a good attitude and the other means a bad attitude."
>
> "Yeah, like that," says Amie.
>
> With their confusion and misconceptions addressed, Carlisle and Jack feel ready to answer the question if they are called on. Mr. Petrites asks for everyone's attention and then calls out "3," which is Carlisle's number. He stands and is able to answer the question and explain his answer when Mr. Petrites calls on him.

Quiz-Quiz-Trade

The final strategy that teachers can use for group responses is called quiz-quiz-trade and is described in *Kagan Cooperative Learning* (Kagan & Kagan, 2009). This strategy is unique because it allows teachers to ask (and students to consider) several questions simultaneously. To prepare for this strategy, each student in the class needs a card with a question on it. So, for example, during the evidence phase of a questioning sequence, each student has already formulated a generalization or conclusion in response to elaboration questions. The teacher then instructs students to think of their conclusion during the activity and passes out cards, each with one of the following questions listed on it:

- What sources support your conclusion?

- What was the reasoning that led you to your conclusion?

- When might your conclusion not be true?

- What errors in reasoning might your conclusion contain?

- What might someone with a different perspective than you think of your conclusion?

Once all students have received a card, they stand up and find a partner. Partner A asks partner B the question on his card, and partner B responds with respect to her conclusion. Then, partner B asks partner A the question on her card, and partner A responds with respect to his own conclusion. Finally, partners switch cards and go find a new partner. The process is repeated with partners switching cards at the end of each interaction. Although a student may have to answer the same question about his own claim twice, this strategy allows each student to hear evidence in support of his peers' claims and practice defending his own claim to several different people. The following vignette depicts this strategy being used in a middle school classroom.

> Ms. Sutton's class has just finished answering elaboration questions about the four quadrants of a coordinate plane. Each student has formulated a conclusion based on his or her answers to elaboration questions. Ms. Sutton passes out a card with an evidence question printed on it to each student and asks everyone to find a partner. Freddie and Nenette pair up, and Freddie asks Nenette the question on his card: What was the reasoning that led you to your conclusion? Since Nenette's conclusion was that the signs of an ordered pair in an odd-numbered quadrant will always match, she quickly sketches a coordinate plane and graphs two ordered pairs, (3, 6) and (−3, −6).
>
> "See," she explains, "by definition, an ordered pair can only be in the first quadrant if both numbers are positive. And an ordered pair can only be in the third quadrant if both numbers are negative. If the signs didn't match, the pair would always end up in the second or fourth quadrant."
>
> Nenette's reasoning makes sense to Freddie, so Nenette asks him the question on her card. After he answers, they switch cards and leave to find new partners.

Group Interaction

When students interact in groups, it is useful if teachers provide guidance about how to function productively while working collaboratively. John Hattie (2009) pointed out that "students can learn most effectively when working together, as it exposes them to multiple perspectives, revision on their thinking, varied explanations for resolving dilemmas, more sources of feedback and correction of errors, and alternative ways to construct knowing" (pp. 225–226). However, he also cautioned that "when the group gets too large, there can be reduced opportunity for individual students to explore their beliefs and hypotheses about what is to be learnt" (p. 226). Therefore, we recommend that teachers limit groups to three to five members during questioning sequences. To help students interact successfully in their groups, the teacher can provide explicit instruction about the interpersonal skills they will need to use. Four strategies that teachers can teach students to use are (1) active listening, (2) conflict resolution, (3) respecting differences, and (4) group reflection.

Active Listening

Active listening is well acknowledged as an important skill for effective interpersonal communication. Overall, the goal of active listening is to absorb a speaker's message, confirm one's understanding to the speaker, and encourage the speaker to express his or her ideas in full. Active listening involves four major components:

1. **Listening for content and emotion** means that the listener pays attention both to what the speaker is saying and to how he is saying it. If a student is expressing his opinion about animal testing in the pharmaceutical industry, those listening to him should listen to what he is saying but also try to gauge whether the opinions he is expressing are strong opinions or weak opinions. If they infer that they are strong opinions, they should try to figure out why he feels so strongly.

2. **Responding to affirm communication** means that the listener communicates back to the speaker to let him know that the message and his emotions about the message have been conveyed. Sometimes this is as simple as nodding one's head. Other times, the listener will briefly paraphrase what he perceives the speaker's message to be. In response to the student speaking about animal testing, another student might say, "It seems as if you feel strongly that harming animals is wrong, especially because of your experience working as an intern at the Humane Society last summer."

3. **Watching for nonverbal cues** means that listeners pay attention to the speaker's body language, verbal inflections, facial expressions, posture, and eye movements. Students listening to their peer talk about animal testing might notice that when he talks about testing potentially lifesaving drugs (rather than cosmetics or pain relievers) on animals, he hesitates more and looks at his hands, as if he is less convicted about his position on animal testing when human life is at stake.

4. **Asking questions** means that listeners give the speaker the opportunity to confirm or deny the listener's perception of his or her message. In the animal testing example, a listener might ask the speaker, "If a potentially lifesaving drug needs to be tested, should an animal's or human's life be put in danger?" This allows the speaker to clarify (or even refine) his position on specific details of the topic at hand.

Students can practice using active listening skills in groups of three. Student A begins by talking about a personally important issue or topic. Student B practices using active listening skills while student A talks. Student C watches student B and makes notes about the active listening skills he sees student B using. After several minutes, student A stops talking, and student C comments on student B's use of active listening skills. Group members then rotate roles (A becomes B, B becomes C, and C becomes A) and repeat the process so that each group member gets a chance to practice and observe active listening.

Conflict Resolution

As students discuss their views and perspectives on various issues, conflicts will inevitably occur. Part of training students to interact effectively in groups involves equipping them with conflict management skills. This requires students to understand the nature of different types of conflict and respond appropriately. A chosen response depends on the circumstances of the conflict and the priorities of the people involved. For example, if the relationship between the two people is important, they may try to minimize the importance of their personal goals in order to preserve the relationship. However, there may be situations in which both issues and relationships are important. David Johnson and Roger Johnson (2005) identified five specific ways to respond to conflict, which are summarized in table 4.1 (page 72).

Table 4.1: Conflict Resolution Strategies

If . . .	Then Use . . .
Goal and relationship are very important	**Negotiating**: Seek solutions that allow both people to achieve their goals while resolving tensions or negative feelings. This may take more time than other strategies and requires each party to be very honest and open about his or her priorities. For example, if your parents want you to pay for your car insurance, but you don't have time to get a job and earn money, you might agree to drive less (to get a lower premium), switch to a cheaper cell phone plan (to free up extra money), and do extra chores around the house (to earn what is still needed for the insurance).
Goal is not important; relationship is very important	**Smoothing**: Let the other person have his or her own way while maintaining a pleasant attitude. For example, if your best friend wants to buy a pink sweater instead of the purple one you think looks better, you might tell her the pink one looks fine to preserve your relationship with her.
Goal is very important; relationship is not important	**Forcing**: Seek to achieve your goal at the other person's expense. When you are forcing, you are less concerned about how the other person feels and more concerned with achieving your goal. For example, when buying a car, people usually focus on getting the best deal possible, regardless of how the salesperson feels.
Goal and relationship are both moderately important	**Compromising**: Give up part of your goals and sacrifice part of the relationship in order to reach an agreement. Compromising is quicker than negotiating and can be used in situations where there is limited time. For example, if your group is creating a PowerPoint and can't agree on the template to use, you might flip a coin and let chance decide which template will be used.
Goal is not important; relationship is not important	**Withdrawing**: Avoid contact with the other person involved in the conflict. For example, if a stranger is rude to you, ignore her and walk away. Withdrawing can also be used as a temporary solution if a conflict has led to a heated situation. For example, all parties involved might agree to leave the issue alone at present and revisit it the next day when everyone is calmer.

Source: Adapted from Johnson & Johnson, 2005.

While some of these strategies (like forcing or smoothing) might seem counterintuitive, each strategy can be useful in specific situations. Teachers can ask students to tell about times in their own lives when each strategy would have been useful or to compose examples of situations where each strategy would be helpful.

Respecting Differences

To help students understand that differences of opinion do not necessarily mean that one party is right and the other party is wrong, teachers can use the following activity (adapted from Garmston & Wellman, 2009). The strategy starts by presenting students with an image such as the one in figure 4.1. Other optical illusions are available at **marzanoresearch.com/classroomstrategies**.

The teacher asks students what the image depicts. Depending on one's perspective, figure 4.1 shows either a young woman or an old lady. After giving students time to respond, the teacher should ask, "Were the people who said 'a young woman' wrong? How about those who said 'an old lady'?" The point of the activity is for students to realize that just because someone sees things differently, it doesn't necessarily mean that person is wrong. To reinforce this point, teachers can suggest that as students work in groups, they try to use the word *and* (which suggests addition and inclusion of ideas) instead of the word *but* (which suggests that the previous speaker was wrong) when discussing issues for which there are several legitimate opinions or points of view. A teacher can also prompt students to use the phrase "I see it a different way" rather than jumping to conclusions about right and wrong.

Group Reflection

After students have finished their group work, they can strengthen their interpersonal skills by reflecting on how well they worked together. To help students reflect on their effectiveness as a group, the teacher can ask groups to think about questions such as the following:

Figure 4.1: Image for Respecting Differences activity.

Source: Hill, 1915.

- What was the purpose of our group's work? Did we accomplish that purpose?

- What questions did our group work raise for us? What problems did we encounter while working as a group?

- How did our performance toward the end of our work together compare to our performance when we started working as a group?

- If we were going to coach others to learn in a group, what could we tell them that would be helpful to them?

Alternatively, the teacher could conduct interviews with groups (using the questions listed here) to keep track of their progress as they work, using a checklist or scoring scale to guide each interview and to help the groups plan their next steps.

Summary

This chapter reviewed strategies that teachers can use to structure and manage students' responses during questioning sequences. Some questions are better suited to students responding individually. Strategies such as chaining and voting, paired response, peer instruction, random names, short written responses, and accuracy checks can help teachers track and respond to individual answers while keeping everyone engaged in the questioning sequence. When students respond in groups, teachers can use strategies such as sticky-note brainstorming, group listing, paired comparisons, numbered heads together, and quiz-quiz-trade to facilitate peer interactions and help students learn from and teach each other. As students work collaboratively, certain skills will help them interact productively and responsively. Active listening, conflict resolution, respecting differences, and group reflection can all be taught explicitly to students, and teachers can prompt them to use these skills during their group interactions.

Chapter 4: Comprehension Questions

1. During what phases of the questioning sequence are you most likely to use individual student response strategies? Group response strategies?

2. Which individual student response strategy are you most likely to try in your classroom? What are its advantages?

3. Which group response strategy are you most likely to try in your classroom? What are its advantages?

4. When might each of the group interaction strategies be particularly helpful in the classroom?

Chapter 5

PREPARATION FOR QUESTIONING SEQUENCES

At its core, a questioning sequence is a fairly straightforward process. As previously explained, a questioning sequence contains four major parts. As a review, these are briefly outlined in table 5.1.

Table 5.1: Four Phases of a Questioning Sequence

Phase	Description
Detail	The teacher asks questions about details important to a topic being addressed in class.
Category	The teacher identifies a category to which the details belong and asks questions regarding the category and its characteristics. Such questions commonly involve: • Asking students to identify examples in the category • Asking students to describe general characteristics of the category • Asking students to make comparisons within and across categories
Elaboration	The teacher asks questions that require students to elaborate on the information identified about a category. Such questions commonly involve: • Asking students to explain reasons for a characteristic (Why? questions) • Asking students to describe the effects of specific characteristics • Asking students to project what might occur under certain circumstances (What if? questions)
Evidence	The teacher asks students to provide evidence that supports their elaborations. Such questions commonly include: • Asking students to identify sources that support their elaborations • Asking students to explain the reasoning they used to construct their elaborations • Asking students to qualify or restrict some of their conclusions • Asking students to find errors in the reasoning used to construct their elaborations • Asking students to examine their elaborations from different perspectives

It is certainly true that a teacher might construct a questioning sequence spontaneously, as an opportunity naturally occurs in class. Consider, for example, a high school physical education teacher who, while introducing the proper procedure for stretching the hamstring muscle before running, thinks of a detail question, such as, Is it better to stretch your hamstring using brief pulsating movements where you stretch and rebound quickly during each movement or to use one long, slow movement where you gradually stretch the muscle and then gradually release?

After a few detail questions like this one, the teacher progresses to the category level. Instead of focusing solely on stretching before running, the teacher asks questions that pertain to the category of preparing for any type of vigorous exercise, such as, How is preparing for running similar to and different from preparing for weight lifting? Students determine that slow, gradual stretches are a good way to prepare for all types of exercise.

Next, the teacher asks an elaboration question, such as, Why is it better to stretch muscles slowly and gradually as opposed to using short, quick stretches? Explain what happens in both situations.

Finally, after students have provided their explanations for the elaboration question, the teacher asks students to identify sources that support their elaborations. He gives them time to look up evidence in their notes and the textbook to support their explanation.

All of this was done without planning on the part of the teacher. The opportunity presented itself, and the questioning sequence seemed to naturally fall together for the teacher. However, whenever possible, such sequences should be planned to maximize their influence on student learning. Specifically, there are two situations a teacher can plan for regarding the use of questioning sequences: (1) questioning sequences that occur within the context of a single lesson and (2) questioning sequences that extend across a number of class periods. Each situation requires different ways of structuring a questioning sequence.

Questioning Sequences Within a Single Lesson

One approach is to plan for a questioning sequence to be used within the confines of a single lesson. Of course, this was the case with the previous example. However, here the teacher takes time to plan for the questioning sequence as opposed to allowing it to occur organically. To illustrate, consider a teacher who is teaching a unit on lines and symmetry. The goal for the unit is that students will draw points, lines, line segments, rays, angles, and perpendicular and parallel lines. During one lesson in that unit, the teacher decides to use a specific questioning sequence. He begins by identifying details that form the basis for the more complex concepts addressed in the unit. He constructs the following detail questions that will be asked right at the beginning of the class:

- What is a point?

- What is a line?

- What is a line segment?

- What is a ray?

- What is an angle?

- What do perpendicular lines look like?

- What do parallel lines look like?

He plans to have students answer these questions using the paired response strategy described in chapter 4.

Next, the teacher selects the category of infinite concepts as a useful one, particularly in helping students understand the implications of perpendicularity. He constructs the following two questions:

- What are examples of geometric concepts that extend to infinity?

- What are characteristics of infinite concepts in geometry?

To answer these questions, the teacher plans to have students work briefly in groups and engage in sticky-note brainstorming.

Additionally, the teacher plans to provide students with options regarding elaboration questions. He constructs the following:

- Why do infinite concepts go on forever?

- What effect do points have on lines?

- What if two lines are neither perpendicular nor parallel?

- What if two rays are perpendicular?

Each student will be asked to select one question to answer or to make up an elaboration question of his or her own. The teacher will allow students to use the Internet to gather information and record their responses on paper.

Finally, the teacher plans to ask all students to respond to the evidence question, What evidence supports your elaborations? Again, students will work individually and can consult the Internet to construct their answers. These responses will be recorded on the same page as the answer to the elaboration question and handed in to the teacher at the end of class. As seen here, it is feasible to plan questioning sequences that occur entirely within a single class period.

Questioning Sequences That Operate Across Multiple Lessons

Although an entire questioning sequence can be conducted within a single class period, it is common for questioning sequences to extend across two or more class periods. This is usually the case when students work in groups or use external sources to answer questions at various phases. As explained in chapter 3, external sources of information can be used at all four phases within a questioning sequence and are very commonly used during the category, elaboration, and evidence phases. Any time a teacher has students use external sources for a phase, it can significantly increase the amount of time that phase will take.

For example, during the category phase of a questioning sequence used in an economics unit that focuses on various economic systems, a teacher has students use the Internet and other external sources to make comparisons between two systems selected from the following list: capitalism, socialism, market economies, mixed economies, planned economies, participatory economies, gift economies, and barter economies. The teacher has students make their comparison selections right after a series of details is addressed. Working individually, the students begin gathering information about the economic systems they have chosen. The entire period the next day might also be devoted to students gathering information to make their comparisons.

Additionally, group work during any phase is another factor that can extend a questioning sequence across multiple lessons. For example, a sticky-note brainstorming activity done in groups could extend to a second day of class to allow adequate time for students to generate conclusions about the characteristics of a category by identifying what is common among all the examples they have generated. In addition to consulting external sources and working in groups, asking students to formally generate and defend claims can extend a questioning sequence across multiple lessons.

Generating and Defending Claims

Having students formally generate and defend claims is an activity that fits well with questioning sequences and invariably requires the sequence to extend across multiple lessons. Although the concept of a claim and the process in which it is defended is implicit in the previous chapters, it is useful to make them explicit. A claim is a new idea or an assertion. Almost by definition, students will generate claims during the elaboration phase of a questioning sequence. There are several types of claims that students can make, as shown in table 5.2.

Table 5.2: Types of Claims

Fact Claims	Fact claims define something or assert that it is true. For example, if a student asserts that the Inuit people eat raw meat, that eating raw meat is associated with parasitic diseases, or that raw meat is a delicacy in certain cultures, she is making a fact claim.
Value Claims	Value claims assert that something is good or bad. For example, if a student asserts that eating raw meat is disgusting or morally wrong, he is making a value claim.
Action Claims	Action claims assert that something should be done. For example, if a student asserts that raw meat should not be eaten in the United States, she is making an action claim.

If students are going to be asked to generate and defend claims explicitly, it is very useful for teachers to explain and exemplify these types to students. Regardless of the form a claim takes, students will need to provide evidence for it.

Evidence

Evidence is already an explicit part of a questioning sequence. When claims are formally generated and defended, a teacher can expand on the nature of evidence. There are three major types of evidence that can support a claim: (1) grounds, (2) backing, and (3) qualifiers. These, too, should be explained and exemplified to students. *Grounds* are the initial evidence for a claim, usually prefaced by the signal word *because*. For example, if a student claims that eating raw meat is bad for you, she might state her claim and her grounds as, "Eating raw meat is bad for you *because* it causes trichinosis." Often, a claim has several grounds; that is, a claim has several reasons that support it. In addition to the grounds previously stated, the student could claim that eating raw meat is bad for you because it can contain E. coli or because it can contain salmonella.

Backing is information about grounds that establishes their validity. There are three types of backing: (1) factual information, (2) expert opinion, and (3) research results. If the student in the previous example wanted to provide factual information to support her grounds that raw meat causes trichinosis, she might refer to an online U.S. Department of Agriculture fact sheet (2011) about *Trichinella spiralis*, the parasite that causes trichinosis. She could paraphrase the fact sheet or use a direct quote, such as "People get trichinellosis (trichinosis) by consuming raw or undercooked meats such as pork, wild boar, bear, bobcat, cougar, fox, wolf, dog, horse, seal, or walrus infected with *Trichinella* larvae." This would be considered factual information. If the student wanted to use expert opinion to support her grounds, she could refer to the opinion of Jean Dupouy-Camet (2000), a microbiologist from Rene Descartes University in Paris, that trichinosis is linked to undercooked meat. Finally, the student could also refer to research results from a clinical study that found that people who consumed raw meat had higher incidences of trichinosis than people who cooked their meat thoroughly (Bălescu, Nemet, Zamfir, Ispas, & Idomir, 2013). Because she is citing the results of a study, this type of backing would be considered research results.

Finally, *qualifiers* tell when a claim might not be true. Consider, for example, the student making the claim that raw meat is associated with parasitic diseases. She qualifies her claim by stating that sushi, when prepared correctly, has many health benefits. She further explains that freezing raw meat for a month will kill parasites, and describes the procedures used in restaurants to ensure that gourmet raw meat dishes (such as steak tartare or ceviche) are free of parasitic microbes.

Errors in Reasoning

As an aspect of generating and defending claims, students can be asked to review their own and each other's collected evidence to determine its relative accuracy and credibility. To help them review evidence, teachers can help students detect errors in reasoning. There are four main types of errors: (1) faulty logic, (2) attack, (3) weak reference, and (4) misinformation. One of the best ways to examine errors in claims is to provide examples of each one. Advertising on television, in print, or on the Internet can provide excellent examples of errors in reasoning.

Errors of faulty logic occur when evidence does not logically support a claim. For example, a student claims that everyone should develop high self-esteem. As grounds for his claim, the student cites a study that found that people with high self-esteem are more likely to marry and raise children.

"Everyone wants to get married and have children, so everyone should develop high self-esteem," he says to his group.

His peers point out that he is using an inaccurate statement, "Everyone wants to get married and have children," to connect his grounds to his claim and is thus committing an error of faulty logic.

Errors of attack occur when irrelevant information is used to support a claim. For example, a student claims that Francis Bacon's philosophy of the human mind is incorrect because he was dismissed from his post as lord chancellor for dishonesty. His peers point out that being dishonest does not necessarily make someone's philosophy wrong. Alternatively, if a student begins his presentation of an expert's opinion by saying, "This guy is super smart. Anyone who disagrees with him is stupid," his peers should point out that he has preemptively attacked anyone who disagrees with the expert he is about to quote.

Errors of weak reference occur when untrustworthy or unreliable sources are used to support a claim. For example, a student claims that the current presidential administration's economic policies favor the rich and victimize the middle class. To support his claim, the student cites a newspaper article about a middle-class family in which both parents lost their jobs, the son was in a car accident, and the daughter found out she had leukemia.

"This is the kind of suffering that the current administration condones," says the student.

His peers point out to him that while the story is very emotionally moving, the current administration's policies had little to do with this particular family's troubles.

Errors of misinformation occur when inaccurate information is used to support a claim. For example, a student claims that high government spending is associated with slow economic growth, citing a study by two Harvard professors showing an average −0.1% growth rate in countries with high government spending. However, a peer who has read the same study, and a correction to the study, alerts the first student to the fact that the Harvard professors based their findings on data that were entered incorrectly into Excel spreadsheets. When the spreadsheets were corrected, high government spending was actually associated with a +2.2% growth rate (Gandel, 2013).

Group Work

When students are working in groups to generate and defend claims, the teacher can help them divide the work of finding appropriate evidence among group members. One of the easiest ways to do this is to identify the claims that a group has generated and assign each claim to a student or students who will seek out evidence for that claim. Each student can then use a template like the one in figure 5.1 to collect evidence.

My claim: _____

_____

Grounds: _____

_____

Backing: _____

_____

Qualifiers: _____

_____

Errors in reasoning in my evidence: _____

_____

Figure 5.1: Evidence-collecting template.

Visit **marzanoresearch.com/classroomstrategies** for a reproducible version of this figure.

Once each student has worked individually to collect grounds, backing, and qualifiers for his or her claim—and has checked the evidence collected to make sure it does not contain any errors in reasoning—the student presents the evidence to his or her group. The group should listen and evaluate each item for accuracy and relevance. Groups can use a scale like the one in table 5.3 to rate each item of evidence collected by group members.

Table 5.3: Rating Scale for Evidence

4	This evidence is solid. It is accurate and relevant.
3	This evidence is good, but I'm not sure it is completely accurate and relevant. It needs to be investigated a bit more.
2	This evidence is iffy. It doesn't seem sufficiently accurate or relevant. This needs to be strengthened or excluded.
1	This evidence isn't appropriate. It either contains errors or isn't relevant. This evidence doesn't really support the claim.

Visit **marzanoresearch.com/classroomstrategies** for a reproducible version of this table.

Groups could also keep their ratings of evidence anonymous. These ratings could then be compiled by the teacher, who reports to the appropriate group members that their evidence needs to be re-examined or strengthened.

Questioning Sequences as the Framework for a Unit

As can be inferred from the previous discussion, a questioning sequence can be the organizational structure for an entire unit. To illustrate, consider an art teacher who designs a unit on impressionism. She spends the first three class periods providing interesting information about impressionist painting along with many examples. She begins her questioning sequence on the third day by asking detail questions about impressionist techniques and category questions about characteristics of impressionist paintings. These phases extend over to the next day as students work in groups. The second week, she begins asking elaboration questions. First, she generates a number of elaboration questions. Then, students are organized into groups, and each group selects one elaboration question to answer. Students are asked to use multiple sources when answering their elaboration questions. Many groups rely heavily on Internet sources along with their textbook and library resources. The teacher allows three class periods for this phase of the sequence. She spends most of her time working with and helping groups. However, she frequently asks groups to make short informal presentations about what they have learned or questions they have about their sources. She also uses these brief interludes to ask some detail questions as a form of review. The latter part of the week is spent with the teacher presenting information designed to clear up some confusion she noticed while working with groups. She also spends time going over the process for generating and defending a claim. The beginning part of the third week is devoted to students formally crafting their claims and providing well-crafted evidence. The unit ends with each group presenting and defending their claims.

General Planning Considerations

Here we consider some general issues teachers can consider to guide their planning efforts as they construct questioning sequences.

Learning Goals

Teachers should ask themselves what information from the learning goal they will use as the focus for their questioning sequence. As explained briefly in chapter 2, questioning sequences should always emanate from the instructional goals that have been established for a unit of instruction. Often, learning goals for a unit come directly from a set of standards. It is important that a teacher analyze standard statements to separate the various aspects of declarative knowledge and procedural skill that students will need to master in order to achieve the standard. To do this, the teacher can use the following sentence stems:

- Students will understand _____.

- Students will be able to _____.

- Students will understand _____ and be able to _____.

Nouns in these statements will frequently indicate information that students need to know or understand, and verbs indicate skills that students need to be able to do. Occasionally, one aspect of a learning goal involves both knowledge and skill. In that case, the third sentence stem is most useful. To illustrate, consider the following goal for a unit on public speaking, taken directly from the Common Core State Standards (CCSS) for English language arts:

SL.7.5: Include multimedia components and visual displays in presentations to clarify claims and findings and emphasize salient points. (NGA & CCSSO, 2010a, p. 49)

Many standards contain several different dimensions of knowledge or skill within one standard. For example, this standard includes:

- Students will know what multimedia components and visual displays are and be able to identify multimedia components and visual displays that could be included in presentations.

- Students will know what claims are and be able to clearly express their claims.

- Students will know what findings are.

- Students will be able to identify salient points.

- Students will be able to select multimedia components and visual displays that clarify claims.

- Students will be able to select multimedia components and visual displays that identify salient points.

- Students will be able to put multimedia components and visual displays in presentations (technical skills).

After deconstructing the standard statement, this teacher decides to focus her questioning sequence on the portion that requires students to select multimedia components and visual displays that identify salient points.

In effect, many aspects of a learning goal or standard can form the basis for a questioning sequence. One of the most important parts of planning is for the teacher to extract a specific aspect of a standard statement that will form the basis of a single questioning sequence.

External Sources

Teachers should also think about which phases, if any, will require students to use external sources and what those sources will be. External sources can be used during any phase of a questioning sequence. Which external sources should be used, and when, are matters of teacher planning. For example, a teacher decides to use the following external sources during the following phases:

- **Detail phase:** Internet

- **Category phase:** video

- **Elaboration phase:** guest speaker

- **Evidence phase:** Supreme Court case

During the detail phase, her students look on the Internet for answers to questions. Students might work individually, in pairs, or in small groups looking up and comparing answers. During the category phase, the teacher shows a video that highlights important characteristics of the focus category. Periodically, she stops the video and has students discuss possible answers for the category questions she asked. For the elaboration phase, the teacher arranges for a guest speaker to join the class to help familiarize students with opinions from various experts in a field. Finally, during the evidence phase, she directs students to the transcript of a Supreme Court case that dealt with the issue at hand. Deciding which external sources to use, acquainting students with the information they need to use them appropriately, and ensuring that students have time to use the information correctly are important matters of teacher planning.

Response Strategies

Another item that teachers should consider when designing a questioning sequence is when students will respond to questions individually and in groups, and what response strategies will be used. Again, individual responses can be used across all phases, as can group responses. Typically, a questioning sequence will involve both types. Teachers should consider the extent to which they want students' answers to be influenced by others when deciding whether to use individual or group responses. Sometimes individual responses are better, other times group responses are better, and in some circumstances, the teacher will want students to answer a question individually before discussing it with their group.

To illustrate, consider a teacher who is using a questioning sequence focused on skip counting. She plans for students to respond individually to detail questions such as the following:

- If you begin at 0 and end at 20, what numbers do you say when you skip count by 2s?

- If you begin at 1 and end at 36, what numbers do you say when you skip count by 5s?

- If you begin at 9 and end at 109, what numbers do you say when you skip count by 10s?

However, when she moves to the category phase, she asks students to work in small groups to answer questions such as:

- What are examples of numbers that have repeating patterns when you use them to skip count?

- What are characteristics of numbers that have repeating patterns when you use them to skip count?

- Compare skip counting by 2s to skip counting by 5s.

- Compare skip counting by 2s to skip counting by 3s.

For the elaboration phase, the teacher asks students to answer one of the following questions individually and write their answers in their academic notebooks:

- Why do numbers that have repeating patterns when you use them to skip count often land on numbers ending in 0?

- What effect does the evenness or oddness of a number have on its skip count pattern?

- What if you skip count by numbers bigger than 10? 100? 1,000?

After students have answered individually, she asks them to form groups of four, compare their answers, and come to an agreement within their groups on an answer to each elaboration question. Finally, during the evidence phase, the existing groups of four respond to questions such as the following:

- What sources can you find to support your group's conclusions?

- How did you figure out your conclusion?

- For numbers that you didn't think formed a pattern, try skip counting higher. Does a pattern show up?

After groups have collected and formulated evidence for their conclusions, each group presents its claims and support to the whole class. Again, careful planning ensures that time and resources necessary for individual and group work are available during the appropriate phases of the questioning sequence.

Generating and Defending Claims

As teachers design questioning sequences, they should consider the extent to which students will be asked to explicitly generate and defend claims. As explained earlier in this chapter, explicitly generating and defending claims is easily inserted in a questioning sequence. The evidence phase of a questioning sequence can be devoted to formally articulating a claim and presenting supporting evidence and appropriate qualifiers. Take, for example, students studying *Candide* who are asked to formulate claims about Voltaire's depiction of optimism in the text. This requires students to read the text, collect textual evidence and inferences, form a claim, and then provide evidence to support that claim.

The process of generating and defending claims can also start at the elaboration phase. Specifically, elaboration questions can be framed to make it clear that the answers to these questions should be formed as claims. For example, the teacher might tell students: Make a claim about how the Lisbon earthquake influenced the ideas expressed in *Candide*. The evidence phase, then, would quite naturally be focused on developing the evidence to support those claims.

Single or Multiple Class Periods

The final consideration that teachers should address is whether a questioning sequence will be executed during a single class period or across multiple class periods. This is usually clear once a teacher has determined:

- The extent to which students will use external sources

- The extent to which teachers will elicit group responses

- The extent to which students will need to generate and defend claims

Extensive use of any of these elements will necessitate multiple class periods. To illustrate, assume a teacher elected to use external sources for each of the four phases of a questioning sequence. By definition, each phase would require time for students to read and analyze new content, which would certainly require multiple class periods. Similarly, if a teacher elected to use group responses during each phase of a questioning sequence, the time needed for the various group interactions would require more than a single class period. Finally, students typically need more than a single class period to generate claims and develop well-crafted arguments.

Summary

Questioning sequences are a powerful tool to help students interact with and deepen new knowledge. However, to maximize their potential, teachers should plan them carefully. Questioning sequences can take place within a single lesson or across multiple lessons. The length of a questioning sequence is often determined by the extent to which students use external sources, respond in groups, and explicitly generate and defend claims. Regardless of the length of a questioning sequence, it should always have a sharp focus derived from a specific learning goal.

Chapter 5: Comprehension Questions

1. How can teachers track students' work during questioning sequences that occur within a single lesson?

2. What are the three types of support for a claim? What are the four types of errors that often occur in evidence?

3. What effect does the use of external sources have on a questioning sequence?

4. What aspects of a questioning sequence should a teacher plan in advance?

EPILOGUE

The basic premise of this book is that logical, intentional, ordered sequences of questions have a far better chance of enhancing student achievement than isolated questions (even "higher-order" ones). Although taxonomies for classifying individual questions are popular in schools, sequencing various types of questions—such as detail, category, elaboration, and evidence questions—is a far more effective way to promote deep understanding and cognition. Rather than avoiding detail questions, the questioning model presented in this book uses them to build a base of factual information that students can subsequently use to answer deeper and more complex questions. As students progress through the questioning sequence, they engage in increasingly complex levels of thinking. During the category phase, they generate lists of examples and identify important characteristics of a category. During the elaboration phase, students use these lists to form claims and conclusions. Finally, in the evidence phase, students engage in argumentation and evaluation as they find evidence to support their claims and revise their conclusions to exclude misconceptions or errors in reasoning.

Teachers who embrace this model of questioning should be able to create questioning experiences in their classrooms that are coherent, logical, and goal driven. Students, too, will see that their answers are leading them toward more complex ideas and perspectives. As they collaborate with peers and share their perspectives and feedback, they take responsibility for their learning. In sum, questioning sequences transform disjointed series of isolated questions into cohesive and harmonious learning experiences.

APPENDIX A

ANSWERS TO COMPREHENSION QUESTIONS

Answers to Chapter 2: Comprehension Questions

1. *Why are detail questions so important to the questioning sequence? What is the most important consideration when designing detail questions?*

   Details are the building blocks of complex ideas and mental constructs. They provide the material for students to use as they engage in higher-order thinking. If students aren't clear about the details of a topic, they will have trouble with more complex questions because they are missing key information. When designing detail questions, teachers should try to draw out what students already know about a topic. Additionally, detail questions can be designed to surface students' misconceptions about a topic so that the teacher can correct them or help students clarify their thinking.

2. *During the category phase, how should teachers select appropriate categories for questioning sequences?*

   The categories that a teacher decides to focus on should be determined by the learning goals for the unit. If the learning goals highlight several categories, the teacher might decide to focus on multiple categories during this phase. If this is the case, the teacher may want to divide students into groups, allowing each group to focus on one category as they proceed into the third and fourth phases of the questioning sequence.

3. *How is the argumentation process incorporated into the elaboration and evidence phases of a questioning sequence?*

   Argumentation, or the process of making and supporting claims, is central to both the elaboration and evidence phases of the questioning sequence. During elaboration, students answer questions about the reasons, effects, and hypothetical outcomes of the characteristics they identified during the category phase. As they answer these questions, they form conclusions or claims about specific categories. Students then support and defend the claims during the evidence phase.

4. *What should students be able to explain about their elaborations or conclusions during the evidence phase?*

   During the evidence phase, students should be able to explain the reasoning they used to construct their elaborations, qualify or restrict some of their conclusions, find errors in their reasoning, and examine their elaborations from different perspectives. Additionally, they should be able to provide sources that support their conclusions.

Answers to Chapter 3: Comprehension Questions

1. *Why is it important for students to be familiar with different linguistic and nonlinguistic text types and structures?*

   When teachers ask questions during questioning sequences, students have two sources of information they can use to answer: their prior knowledge and external sources. As students consult external sources (both print and electronic), they will encounter different text structures and document types. Knowing what to expect from each structure or type will help them quickly identify information to help them answer a question. Additionally, familiarity with various structures and types allows students to detect potential author biases or missing information.

2. *Describe the five linguistic text structures reviewed in this chapter, and explain how students can identify them.*

   The five linguistic text structures are (1) description, (2) sequence, (3) causation, (4) problem/solution, and (5) comparison. Description structures give information about a topic by highlighting its characteristics, attributes, or identifying marks and are signaled by words and phrases such as *attributes, characteristics, for example, for instance, namely, specifically,* and *such as.* Sequence structures organize a series of events in chronological order. Time words and phrases such as *before, after, later, previously, early, finally, following, next, years ago,* and so forth signal sequence structures. Causation structures present cause-and-effect relationships, using signal words and phrases such as *consequently, as a result, in order to, the reason, this is why,* and so on. Problem/solution structures present problems and potential solutions; sometimes problem/solution structures feature questions and answers. Signal words and phrases such as *problem, solution, question, answer, response, satisfy, issue, prevent,* and *solve* alert students to the use of a problem/solution structure. Finally, comparison structures highlight the similarities and differences between two items or ideas. Words and phrases such as *although, compared to, difference, in common, in contrast, instead,* and *on the other hand* can help students identify comparison structures.

3. *How can teachers help students practice identifying and interpreting nonlinguistic texts?*

   As teachers introduce various types of matrix, graphic, and mimetic texts, they can ask students to find examples of each type of text and bring them to class. Then, the class can analyze each one to decide which subcategory it fits into (for example, Is it a simple, combined, intersecting, or nested list? Is it a pie chart, bar or line graph, or map? Is it a picture or schematic?), what information it is communicating, and how it might communicate bias or reinforce misconceptions.

4. *How are electronic texts similar to and different from linguistic and nonlinguistic texts?*

   Like traditional linguistic and nonlinguistic texts, which are usually printed on static pages, electronic texts are usually organized using recognizable structures. Students who know these structures can use them as they read electronic texts to help them know what to look for and remember in each type of text. However, electronic texts differ from traditional linguistic and nonlinguistic texts because they are usually displayed on a screen, are read by scrolling up or down rather than by turning pages, and can be resized and reshaped depending on the size and orientation of the screen. These unique features mean that students will need to focus more time and energy on electronic texts, or use strategies (such as printing them out) that make it possible to read electronic texts like traditional print texts. Additionally, electronic texts require a more extensive set of comprehension skills, and the ability to distinguish relevant from irrelevant information.

5. *How can teachers help students find and synthesize information from multiple texts?*

First, teachers help students clearly identify what they are looking for. This could involve generating keywords or narrowing searches to focus precisely on the information students need. Teachers can also help students identify the elements of the answer that they already know and what information they still need to find. As students conduct research, teachers can help them revisit their focus and continually refine their search.

Answers to Chapter 4: Comprehension Questions

1. *During what phases of the questioning sequence are you most likely to use individual student response strategies? Group response strategies?*

   Although individual and group responses can be used during any phase of the questioning sequence, individual responses may be most useful during the detail and category phases. Group responses are particularly suited to the elaboration and evidence phases, when students may have to address and respond to diverse perspectives and opinions about their conclusions for various issues.

2. *Which individual student response strategy are you most likely to try in your classroom? What are its advantages?*

   Answers will vary. Response chaining and voting are advantageous because they allow the teacher to call on multiple students to answer each question, creating a class discussion rather than a simple back-and-forth exchange. Paired response allows students to rehearse their responses before sharing with the entire class. Peer instruction is beneficial because students defend their answers to one another and can change their answers based on the arguments of their peers. Choosing random names keeps all students on their toes, since no one knows who will be called on next, and short written responses allow students and the teacher to keep a record of their learning. Similarly, accuracy checks keep all students engaged, even if they aren't currently answering a question, and sharpen their skill in finding and checking information on the Internet.

3. *Which group response strategy are you most likely to try in your classroom? What are its advantages?*

   Answers will vary. Sticky-note brainstorming helps students generate many ideas at once, which can be particularly helpful during the category phase of a questioning sequence. Generating lists of examples and characteristics of those examples will help students during subsequent phases. Group listing also helps students generate ideas but goes a step further by asking students to rank their ideas by order of importance. Paired comparisons get students up and moving, which leads to increased engagement and allows students to refine their answers as they confer with other students. Numbered heads together gives students an opportunity to learn from each other and keeps all students engaged since no one knows which number will be called. Finally, quiz-quiz-trade allows students to consider several questions at once. This is particularly useful during the evidence phase, when students need practice defending their conclusions to people with various (and possibly opposing) perspectives.

4. *When might each of the group interaction strategies be particularly helpful in the classroom?*

   Active listening is a lifelong skill that not only communicates respect and appreciation for a speaker but also involves the listener more deeply in a discussion. If students aren't sure what they have to contribute to a discussion, actively listening to others' ideas can prompt them to think of new perspectives or related issues that they want to bring up. Similarly, conflict resolution skills will help students throughout their lives. When working in groups, students often disagree about small issues that can be solved through smoothing or compromise. When discussing larger, more controversial issues, students may need to use problem-solving negotiations to formulate conclusions with which everyone can agree. Respecting differences allows students to disagree with their peers without communicating disrespect or disregard. Using *and* instead of *but* is a simple strategy that can change the tone of students' conversations. Finally, group reflection allows students to step back and talk about their interactions, identifying attitudes that are productive or counterproductive and ways they can work better together.

Answers to Chapter 5: Comprehension Questions

1. *How can teachers track students' work during questioning sequences that occur within a single lesson?*

   Teachers can use academic notebooks or sheets of paper to track students' work during a questioning sequence. Since questioning sequences that occur within a single lesson often do not involve extended research in external sources or extensive development of claims and evidence, students can simply write down their claims on a piece of paper and then list evidence that supports those elaborations. These can be kept in students' academic notebooks or turned in to the teacher at the end of class.

2. *What are the three types of support for a claim? What are the four types of errors that often occur in evidence?*

   Claims are supported with grounds, backing, and qualifiers. Grounds are the reasons one believes a claim to be true and are often signaled by the word *because*. Backing provides information about why the grounds are true. There are three types of backing: (1) factual information, (2) expert opinion, and (3) research results. Qualifiers are exceptions to a claim; they explain instances or circumstances under which a claim might not be true. The four types of errors that occur in evidence are (1) errors of faulty logic, (2) errors of attack, (3) errors of weak reference, and (4) errors of misinformation.

3. *What effect does the use of external sources have on a questioning sequence?*

   Typically, the use of external sources requires a questioning sequence to extend beyond a single class period. Since students need to time to find, read, and gather information from external sources, teachers will often begin a questioning sequence in one class, allow students time to consult external sources between classes, and continue the questioning sequence during class the next day.

4. *What aspects of a questioning sequence should a teacher plan in advance?*

   First and foremost, a teacher should identify the focus of a questioning sequence by analyzing the specific aspects of knowledge and skill articulated in a standard or learning goal. Then, the teacher should consider the extent to which students will consult external sources, the extent to which students will be asked to formally generate and defend claims, and when students will work individually and in groups during a questioning sequence. These three aspects (consulting external sources, generating and defending claims, and working in groups) will likely extend the questioning sequence across multiple class periods. When planning questioning sequences that extend across several class periods, the teacher should determine which phases will occur during which class periods and how much time will be allotted for students to engage in extended tasks related to the questioning sequence.

APPENDIX B

EXAMPLES OF QUESTIONING SEQUENCES

As explained in chapter 2 and expanded on in chapter 5, questioning sequences should always be tied to a learning goal or a standard. However, standards are often stated in such a way as to include a wide range of knowledge and skills, which teachers must separate to create questioning sequences that focus on just one aspect of knowledge or skill contained in a standard. For example, consider the following math standard.

> 2.NBT.A.3: Read and write numbers to 1000 using base-ten numerals, number names, and expanded form. (NGA & CCSSO, 2010c, p. 19)

When this standard is broken down into its component parts, it becomes clear that it involves many aspects of knowledge and skill. For example:

- Students will understand what base-ten numerals are.

- Students will understand the names for all the numbers to 1,000.

- Students will understand what expanded form is.

- Students will be able to write every digit from 1 to 9.

Additionally, teachers should consider knowledge and skills that are not explicit in a standard but are important prerequisites to achieving the standard, such as:

- Students will understand how place value works.

- Students will be able to use knowledge of place value to arrange digits in multidigit numbers.

- Students will understand addition and how it relates to expanded form.

This list is not exhaustive, and there are certainly other aspects of knowledge and skill that are part of this standard. To use questioning sequences effectively, teachers must identify which aspect of a standard they are focusing on. For example, a teacher could choose to focus a questioning sequence on the physical action of writing digits from 1 to 9, the human construct of place value, or the mental action of addition. As shown here, there are many options for the focus of a questioning sequence. Teachers should feel free to use their judgment when identifying the focus for their questioning sequences.

Structure and Format of Example Sequences

In the following examples covering a variety of subject areas and all grade levels (arranged chronologically), we provide a standard statement from the Common Core State Standards or Next Generation Science Standards (NGSS), several aspects of knowledge and skill from the standard that could be the focus of a questioning sequence, and a questioning sequence based on one of those aspects. Keep in mind that the examples in this appendix are offered to demonstrate the flexibility and adaptability of the questioning sequence. Teachers should use these examples as a reference for designing their own questioning sequences related to their goals.

Teachers will notice in the following examples that the questions in the detail and category phases do not always directly match the wording of the question stems from tables 2.1 and 2.2 (pages 17 and 21). This is because those stems are meant to suggest a starting point, from which questions should be adapted to suit various grade levels and content areas. In the following questioning sequences, questions have been written in student-friendly language appropriate for the designated grade level. At the beginning of the detail phase of each questioning sequence, the type of detail (from table 2.1) being focused on appears in bold. After select student-friendly questions in the detail and category phases, we have included a prompt word in parentheses—for example, "(*process*)"—to let teachers know which stem from table 2.1 or 2.2 (also indicated in italics) was used to design the question. Additionally, when we give example comparison questions in the category phase, we alert readers to the type of comparison and the categories being compared with a parenthetical phrase such as "(within-category comparison—vowels)" or "(across-category comparison—vowel to consonant)."

Note that not all of the detail and category questions in the following examples include parenthetical prompt words. The stems in tables 2.1 and 2.2 are meant to help teachers if they are having trouble composing detail or category questions, but teachers should also feel free to design questions that are not directly linked to the types and prompt words in tables 2.1 and 2.2.

Organization and Notation of Standards

When we reference a standard from the CCSS or the NGSS, we use the notation system preferred by the standards' authors. For the CCSS, we use a simplified version of the *dot notation system*. Explanations of the standards notation for English language arts (ELA), mathematics, and science follow.

English Language Arts

For ELA standards, the first set of initials in the notation refers to which of the four strands the standard belongs to (with the Reading strand being further separated into three distinct parts):

- Reading

  - Literature = RL
  - Informational Text = RI
  - Foundational Skills = RF

- Writing = W

- Speaking and Listening = SL

- Language = L

The number (or in the case of kindergarten, the letter) following the first period indicates the grade level of the standard, and the final number or range of numbers indicates the specific standard or standards at that grade level. Therefore, RL.5.3, for example, indicates the third standard for fifth grade in reading literature.

Mathematics

For K–8 mathematics, the initial number indicates the grade level of the standard. The initials following the first period indicate the domain of the standard:

- Counting and cardinality = CC

- Operations and algebraic thinking = OA

- Number and operations in base ten = NBT

- Number and operations—fractions = NF

- Measurement and data = MD

- Geometry = G

- Ratios and proportional relationships = RP

- The number system = NS

- Expressions and equations = EE

- Statistics and probability = SP

- Functions = F

The final letter (A, B, C, or D) and number indicate the standard's cluster and number. Therefore, 2.NBT.A.3, for example, indicates the third standard in the first cluster (A) in the domain of number and operations in base ten for second grade.

High school standards are denoted with "HS," followed by initials for one of five conceptual categories, a dash, and an additional set of initials to indicate the domain within that category, as follows:

- Number and Quantity = HSN

  - The real number system = HSN-RN

  - Quantities = HSN-Q

  - The complex number system = HSN-CN

- Algebra = HSA

  - Seeing structure in expressions = HSA-SSE

  - Arithmetic with polynomials and rational expressions = HSA-APR

  - Creating equations = HSA-CED

  - Reasoning with equations and inequalities = HSA-REI

- Functions = HSF

    - Interpreting functions = HSF-IF

    - Building functions = HSF-BF

    - Linear, quadratic, and exponential models = HSF-LE

    - Trigonometric functions = HSF-TF

- Geometry = HSG

    - Congruence = HSG-CO

    - Similarity, right triangles, and trigonometry = HSG-SRT

    - Circles = HSG-C

    - Expressing geometric properties with equations = HSG-GPE

    - Geometric measurement and dimension = HSG-GMD

    - Modeling with geometry = HSG-MG

- Statistics and Probability = HSS

    - Interpreting categorical and quantitative data = HSS-ID

    - Making inferences and justifying conclusions = HSS-IC

    - Conditional probability and the rules of probability = HSS-CP

    - Using probability to make decisions = HSS-MD

As with the K–8 standards, the final letter and number indicate the standard's cluster and number. So, HSF-IF.C.7, for example, denotes the seventh standard in the third cluster (C) in the domain of interpreting functions for the high school conceptual category of functions.

Science

For the NGSS, the letters or number before the dash indicate the grade level of the standard (MS indicates middle school, and HS indicates high school). The alphanumeric code after the dash indicates the core idea of the standard:

- Physical science = PS

- Life sciences = LS

- Earth and space sciences = ESS

- Engineering, technology, and applications of science = ETS

The number included in the alphanumeric code identifies the specific core idea (there are four core ideas in physical science, four in the life sciences, three in earth and space sciences, and two in engineering, technology, and applications of science). The final number indicates a specific standard within that core idea. Therefore, 4-ESS2-1, for example, indicates the first standard for the second core idea in earth and space sciences for fourth grade.

Kindergarten Reading

Consider the following English language arts standards.

RF.K.3a–3b: Demonstrate basic knowledge of one-to-one letter-sound correspondences by producing the primary sound or many of the most frequent sounds for each consonant.

Associate the long and short sounds with common spellings (graphemes) for the five major vowels. (NGA & CCSSO, 2010a, p. 16)

A teacher using this standard in a questioning sequence could focus on the following:

- Students will understand what sound or sounds are associated with each letter.

- Students will be able to produce the sound or sounds for each letter.

In this example, we focus on being able to produce the sound or sounds for each letter.

Details

To begin the questioning sequence, the teacher asks questions about the **physical action** of pronouncing sounds.

- What sound(s) does A make? B? C? and so on.

- What does your mouth do when you make the A sound? B sound? C sound? and so on. (*process*)

- How do you know which sound to make if a letter has two sounds, like C or G? (*cause or consequence*)

Category

Teachers should select a category or categories based on their focus for a unit. In this example, the teacher focuses questions on two categories: vowels and consonants.

Ask students to identify examples within a category:

- What vowels do you know?

- What consonants do you know?

Ask students to describe the general characteristics of a category:

- What things do A, E, I, O, and U have in common or share?

- What things do B, D, and P (and other groups of consonants) have in common or share?

- What does your mouth do when you make a vowel sound? (*process*)

- What does your mouth do when you make a consonant sound? (*process*)

Ask students to make comparisons within and across categories:

- How is A like U? How is A different from U? (within-category comparison—vowels)

- How is O like D? How is O different from D? (across-category comparison—vowel to consonant)

- How is O like DOG? How is O different from DOG? (across-category comparison—vowel to word)

Elaboration

Elaboration questions build on students' answers to category questions. Therefore, the teacher uses students' responses to category questions to construct elaboration questions.

Ask students to explain reasons for characteristics (Why? questions):

- Why do you have to open your mouth to make a vowel sound?

Ask students to describe the effects of specific characteristics:

- What happens when you put vowels and consonants together?

Ask students to project what might occur under certain conditions (What if? questions):

- What if you try to pronounce a vowel with your mouth closed?

- What if a word doesn't have any vowels in it?

Evidence

If students conclude that vowels make you open your mouth and consonants make you close your mouth, and consonants and vowels work together to make words, the teacher can prompt students to provide evidence for their conclusions.

Ask students to explain the reasoning they used to construct their elaborations:

- How did you figure out that vowels make you open your mouth?

- How did you figure out that consonants make you close your mouth?

Ask students to qualify or restrict some of their conclusions:

- What about the letter Y? Is it a vowel or a consonant?

Grade 1 Science

Consider the following science standard.

> 1-PS4-1: Plan and conduct investigations to provide evidence that vibrating materials can make sound and that sound can make materials vibrate. (Achieve, 2013, p. 11)

A teacher using this standard in a questioning sequence could focus on the following:

- Students will be able to plan investigations.

- Students will be able to conduct investigations.

- Students will understand what evidence is and be able to provide it.

- Students will understand that sounds are vibrations.

In this example, we focus on understanding that sounds are vibrations.

Details

To begin the questioning sequence, the teacher asks students about the **natural phenomenon** of vibration.

- What sorts of things vibrate?

- What happens when something vibrates? (*happened/happens*)

- Do things vibrate fast or slow?

- How long do things vibrate for?

Category

Teachers should select a category or categories based on their focus for a unit. In this example, the teacher focuses questions on two categories: things that make sound when they vibrate and things that vibrate in response to sounds.

Ask students to identify examples within a category:

- What sorts of things make sound when they vibrate?

- What sorts of things vibrate when there are loud sounds?

Ask students to describe the general characteristics of a category:

- What do the things that make sound when they vibrate have in common or share?

- What do the things that vibrate when there are loud sounds have in common or share?

- What do you have to do to make something start vibrating and making sound? (*causes or consequences*)

- Where do you find things that vibrate when there are loud sounds? (*places*)

Ask students to make comparisons within and across categories:

- Compare a string to a tuning fork. (within-category comparison—things that make sound when they vibrate)

- Compare a tuning fork to water. (across-category comparison—things that make sound when they vibrate to things that vibrate in response to sounds)

Elaboration

Elaboration questions build on students' answers to category questions. Therefore, the teacher uses students' responses to category questions to construct elaboration questions.

Ask students to explain reasons for characteristics (Why? questions):

- Why do things make sound when they vibrate?

- Why can sound make certain materials vibrate?

Ask students to describe the effects of specific characteristics:

- What do sounds do to air? To water? To solid things (like dirt or walls)?

Ask students to project what might occur under certain conditions (What if? questions):

- What if you listen to sounds through the air? Through water? Through solid things (like dirt or walls)?

Evidence

If students conclude that sounds move more easily through materials that vibrate easily (like a string or a piece of wood), the teacher can prompt students to provide evidence for their conclusions.

Ask students to explain the reasoning they used to construct their elaborations:

- How did you figure that out?

Ask students to qualify or restrict some of their conclusions:

- Are there ever times when vibrations don't make sound?

- Why do windows break when there are loud sounds?

Ask students to examine their elaborations from different perspectives:

- How do you hear things? What vibrates in your head?

- Why can't deaf people hear sounds?

Grade 2 Mathematics

Consider the following mathematics standard.

> 2.OA.C.3: Determine whether a group of objects (up to 20) has an odd or even number of members, e.g., by pairing objects or counting them by 2s; write an equation to express an even number as a sum of two equal addends. (NGA & CCSSO, 2010c, p. 19)

A teacher using this standard in a questioning sequence could focus on the following:

- Students will be able to count a group of objects.

- Students will understand which numbers are even and which are odd.

- Students will be able to pair up groups of objects.

- Students will understand that if a group of objects can be paired evenly, it has an even number of items.

- Students will understand that if a group of objects has a leftover after being paired, it has an odd number of items.

- Students will be able to identify groups of objects as having an even or odd number of objects.

- Students will understand that even numbers can be composed by adding a number to itself (doubling) and will be able to figure out which addend can be added to itself to equal a specific even number.

In this example, we focus on understanding which numbers are even and which are odd.

Details

To begin the questioning sequence, the teacher asks students about the **human constructs** of even and odd numbers.

- Is 1 even or odd? 2? 3? and so on.

- What pattern do even and odd numbers make when you count? (*measurement, quantity, or quality*)

- Why are even numbers helpful? Odd numbers? (*organize the world*)

Category

Teachers should select a category or categories based on their focus for a unit. In this example, the teacher focuses questions on two categories: even numbers and odd numbers.

Ask students to identify examples within a category:

- Which numbers between 1 and 10 are even? Which are odd?

Ask students to describe the general characteristics of a category:

- What do all the even numbers have in common? The odd numbers?

- What are even numbers used for? Odd numbers? (*purpose*)

- What numbers do you add to make even numbers? Odd numbers? (*causes or consequences*)

Ask students to make comparisons within and across categories:

- Compare 1 to 11. (within-category comparison—odd numbers)

- Compare 3 to 4. (across-category comparison—odd number to even number)

Elaboration

Elaboration questions build on students' answers to category questions. Therefore, the teacher uses students' responses to category questions to construct elaboration questions.

Ask students to explain reasons for characteristics (Why? questions):

- Why do odd numbers make leftovers?

- Why are even numbers fairer?

Ask students to describe the effects of specific characteristics:

- What effect does the number you start with have on skip counting?

Ask students to project what might occur under certain conditions (What if? questions):

- What if you skip count by an odd number? By an even number?

Evidence

If students conclude that starting with an even number and skip counting by an even number makes you land on even numbers; starting with an odd number and skip counting by an even number makes you land on odd numbers; starting with an even number and skip counting by an odd number makes you land on an odd number, then an even number, then an odd number, and so on; and starting with an odd number and skip counting by an odd number makes you land on an even number, then an odd number, then an even number, and so on, the teacher can prompt students to provide evidence for their conclusions.

Ask students to explain the reasoning they used to construct their elaborations:

- How did you figure out that the starting number and the skip count number affect whether you land on odd or even numbers?

Ask students to qualify or restrict some of their conclusions:

- Is zero odd or even?

Ask students to examine their elaborations from different perspectives:

- Would your system still work if one of the numbers (like 9) was missing?

Grade 3 Writing

Consider the following English language arts standards.

> W.3.1: Write opinion pieces on topics or texts, supporting a point of view with reasons.
>
> a. Introduce the topic or text they are writing about, state an opinion, and create an organizational structure that lists reasons.
>
> b. Provide reasons that support the opinion.
>
> c. Use linking words and phrases (e.g., *because, therefore, since, for example*) to connect opinion and reasons.
>
> d. Provide a concluding statement or section. (NGA & CCSSO, 2010a, p. 20)

A teacher using this standard in a questioning sequence could focus on the following:

- Students will understand what an opinion is.

- Students will be able to write opinion pieces.

- Students will be able to introduce a topic.

- Students will understand what an organizational structure is and will be able to choose an organizational structure that lists reasons.

- Students will understand what support is and be able to choose reasons that support an opinion.

- Students will understand what linking words and phrases are and be able to use them to connect opinions with reasons.

- Students will understand what a concluding section should do and will be able to write a concluding statement or section.

In this example, we focus on understanding what an opinion is.

Details

To begin the questioning sequence, the teacher asks students about opinion, which is considered a **feeling, condition, or state**.

- What do you do when you have an opinion? (*actions*)

- What makes you have an opinion about something? (*causes or consequences*)

- Are opinions important? (*value*)

- How do people's opinions change? (*arrive at*)

- Do opinions ever lead to bad consequences? (*dangers*)

Category

Teachers should select a category or categories based on their focus for a unit. In this example, the teacher focuses questions on two categories: opinions and facts.

Ask students to identify examples within a category:

- What are some examples of opinions you have or you've heard other people say?

- What are examples of facts you know?

Ask students to describe the general characteristics of a category:

- What do all of the opinions you listed have in common?

- What do all of the facts you listed have in common?

- How do people form opinions? (*process*)

- How do people find out about facts? (*process*)

- What makes people form an opinion about something? (*causes or consequences*)

- What makes people find out facts about something? (*causes or consequences*)

Ask students to make comparisons within and across categories:

- Compare your opinion to someone else's opinion on a topic. (within-category comparison—opinions)

- Compare your opinion to a set of facts about a topic. (across-category comparison—opinion to facts)

Elaboration

Elaboration questions build on students' answers to category questions. Therefore, the teacher uses students' responses to category questions to construct elaboration questions.

Ask students to explain reasons for characteristics (Why? questions):

- Why do people base their opinions on how they feel about a topic?

- Why do people usually form opinions after hearing information about a topic?

Ask students to describe the effects of specific characteristics:

- What effect do facts have on people's opinions?

- What effect do opinions have on how people think?

Ask students to project what might occur under certain conditions (What if? questions):

- What if people always based their opinions on facts?

Evidence

If students conclude that people would always agree if they based their opinions on facts, the teacher can prompt students to provide evidence for their conclusions.

Ask students to qualify or restrict some of their conclusions:

- Has anyone ever shown the same two people one set of facts and then studied whether their opinions agree?

Ask students to find errors in the reasoning used to construct their elaborations:

- If you and your friend look at a set of facts, do you always agree about what should be done?

Ask students to examine their elaborations from different perspectives:

- Why do smart people who look at the facts still disagree sometimes?

Grade 4 Science

Consider the following science standard.

> 4-ESS2-1: Make observations and/or measurements to provide evidence of the effects of weathering or the rate of erosion by water, ice, wind, or vegetation. (Achieve, 2013, p. 35)

A teacher using this standard in a questioning sequence could focus on the following:

- Students will be able to make observations.

- Students will be able to make measurements.

- Students will understand what evidence is and be able to provide evidence.

- Students will understand what weathering is and will be able to recognize the effects of weathering.

- Students will understand what erosion is and be able to recognize erosion.

- Students will understand how water, ice, and wind affect erosion.

- Students will understand how vegetation affects erosion.

In this example, we focus on understanding how water, ice, and wind affect erosion.

Details

To begin the questioning sequence, the teacher asks students about the **natural phenomenon** of erosion.

- Where does erosion happen? (*places*)

- How long does erosion take? (*time*)

- What problems can erosion cause? (*causes or consequences*)

- What happens during erosion? (*happened/happens*)

Category

Teachers should select a category or categories based on their focus for a unit. In this example, the teacher focuses questions on three categories: water erosion, ice erosion, and wind erosion.

Ask students to identify examples within a category:

- What places show examples of water erosion? Ice erosion? Wind erosion?

Ask students to describe the general characteristics of a category:

- What do all the examples of water erosion that you listed have in common? Examples of ice erosion? Examples of wind erosion?

- What happens during water erosion? Ice erosion? Wind erosion? (*process*)

- What happens because of water erosion? Ice erosion? Wind erosion? (*causes or consequences*)

- Where does water erosion happen? Ice erosion? Wind erosion? (*places*)

Ask students to make comparisons within and across categories:

- Compare gully erosion to shoreline erosion. (within-category comparison—water erosion)

- Compare bank erosion to abrasion. (across-category comparison—water erosion to wind erosion)

Elaboration

Elaboration questions build on students' answers to category questions. Therefore, the teacher uses students' responses to category questions to construct elaboration questions.

Ask students to explain reasons for characteristics (Why? questions):

- Why does gully erosion get worse over time?

- Why is water erosion most likely in places that get a lot of rain?

Ask students to describe the effects of specific characteristics:

- How does deforestation affect erosion?

- How does farming affect erosion?

Ask students to project what might occur under certain conditions (What if? questions):

- What if soil or rocks erode away from under a bank to create an overhang?

Evidence

If students conclude that deforestation is a major contributor to water erosion, the teacher can prompt students to provide evidence for their conclusions.

Ask students to identify sources that support their elaborations:

- What sources support your claim?

- What measurements support your claim?

- What observations support your claim?

Ask students to explain the reasoning they used to construct their elaborations:

- How did you figure out that deforestation contributes to water erosion?

Ask students to qualify or restrict some of their conclusions:

- Is there ever a time when deforestation prevents water erosion?

Ask students to find errors in the reasoning used to construct their elaborations:

- What benefits come from deforestation?

Ask students to examine their elaborations from different perspectives:

- How might one obtain the benefits of harvesting lumber without the drawbacks of erosion and deforestation?

Grade 5 Reading

Consider the following English language arts standard.

> RL.5.3: Compare and contrast two or more characters, settings, or events in a story or drama, drawing on specific details in the text (e.g., how characters interact). (NGA & CCSSO, 2010a, p. 12)

A teacher using this standard in a questioning sequence could focus on the following:

- Students will understand what a story is.

- Students will understand what a drama is.

- Students will be able to compare and contrast characters in a text.

- Students will be able to compare and contrast settings in a text.

- Students will be able to compare and contrast events in a text.

- Students will be able to identify specific details in a text.

- Students will be able to use details to compare and contrast.

In this example, we focus on comparing and contrasting characters in a text.

Details

To begin the questioning sequence, the teacher asks students about specific characters (**people**) in a text. For this example, the text being used is *Bud, Not Buddy* by Christopher Paul Curtis.

- When did Bud Caldwell live? (*time period*)

- Where does Herman E. Calloway live? (*places*)

- Where does Bud meet Deza Malone? (*places*)

- Where does Todd Amos live? (*places*)

- What happens when Bud meets Lefty Lewis? (*events*)

- What is Miss Grace Thomas famous for? (*accomplishments*)

Category

Teachers should select a category or categories based on their focus for a unit. In this example, the teacher focuses questions on three categories: people who help Bud, people who hurt or don't help Bud, and people Bud helps.

Ask students to identify examples within a category:

- What are examples of people who help Bud? People who hurt or don't help Bud? People Bud helps?

Ask students to describe the general characteristics of a category:

- What are people who help Bud like? People who hurt or don't help Bud? People Bud helps?

- What do people who help Bud do? People who hurt or don't help Bud? People Bud helps? (*actions*)

- What do people who help Bud look like? People who hurt or don't help Bud? People Bud helps? (*physical traits*)

- What thoughts or attitudes are common to people who help Bud? People who hurt or don't help Bud? People Bud helps? (*psychological traits*)

Ask students to make comparisons within and across categories:

- Compare Lefty Lewis to Steady Eddie. (within-category comparison—people who help Bud)

- Compare Bud's pretend mother and father at the mission to the Amoses. (across-category comparison—people who help Bud to people who hurt or don't help Bud)

Elaboration

Elaboration questions build on students' answers to category questions. Therefore, the teacher uses students' responses to category questions to construct elaboration questions.

Ask students to explain reasons for characteristics (Why? questions):

- Why are the adults who listen to Bud and think about him the same people who help him?

Ask students to describe the effects of specific characteristics:

- What effect does being treated like a responsibility, object, or nuisance have on Bud?

Ask students to project what might occur under certain conditions (What if? questions):

- What if Herman E. Calloway had treated Bud like a nuisance instead of listening to him?

Evidence

If students conclude that Herman E. Calloway would have missed out on discovering what happened to his daughter and grandson if he had treated Bud like a nuisance, but that his kindness actually benefitted him, the teacher can prompt students to provide evidence for their conclusions.

Ask students to identify sources that support their elaborations:

- What passages in the book support your claim?

Ask students to qualify or restrict some of their conclusions:

- Are there any times when Herman E. Calloway does treat Bud like a nuisance?

Ask students to examine their elaborations from different perspectives:

- What might a different perspective of Herman E. Calloway's actions be?

Grade 6 Writing

Consider the following English language arts standard.

> W.6.4: Produce clear and coherent writing in which the development, organization, and style are appropriate to task, purpose, and audience. (NGA & CCSSO, 2010a, p. 43)

A teacher using this standard in a questioning sequence could focus on the following:

- Students will be able to write clearly and coherently.

- Students will understand what development, organization, and style are.

- Students will understand the task or purpose for their writing and be able to write appropriately for it.

- Students will understand the audience for their writing and be able to write appropriately for it.

In this example, we focus on understanding the audience for a piece of writing.

Details

To begin the questioning sequence, the teacher asks students about different **groups or organizations** who might be audiences for their writing.

- What beliefs might an audience of other students have? An audience of parents? An audience of teachers? (*beliefs*)

- Where might an audience of other students read your writing? An audience of parents? An audience of teachers? (*locations*)

- When might an audience of other students read your writing? An audience of parents? An audience of teachers? (*time period*)

- What might an audience of other students be doing while they read your writing? An audience of parents? An audience of teachers? (*events*)

Category

Teachers should select a category or categories based on their focus for a unit. In this example, the teacher focuses questions on one category: sympathetic audiences.

Ask students to identify examples within a category:

- What are examples of sympathetic audiences?

Ask students to describe the general characteristics of a category:

- Why might a sympathetic audience read what you wrote? (*purpose*)

- Who might be a member of a sympathetic audience? (*people*)

- Where might you encounter a sympathetic audience? (*places*)

Ask students to make comparisons within and across categories:

- Compare your parents as an audience to your best friend as an audience. (within-category comparison—sympathetic audiences)

- Compare your parents as an audience to a student who doesn't like you as an audience. (across-category comparison—sympathetic audience to hostile audience)

Elaboration

Elaboration questions build on students' answers to category questions. Therefore, the teacher uses students' responses to category questions to construct elaboration questions.

Ask students to explain reasons for characteristics (Why? questions):

- Why are people who like you usually sympathetic audiences?

- Why might someone who doesn't like you not listen to you very carefully?

Ask students to describe the effects of specific characteristics:

- What effect does an unsympathetic audience have on how much evidence you present?

- What effect does a sympathetic audience have on how carefully you construct an argument?

Ask students to project what might occur under certain conditions (What if? questions):

- What might happen if something written for a sympathetic audience was shown to a hostile audience?

Evidence

If students conclude that it is crucial to know your audience before you write a piece, the teacher can prompt students to provide evidence for their conclusions.

Ask students to identify sources that support their elaborations:

- What sources do you have to support your claim?

Ask students to explain the reasoning they used to construct their elaborations:

- How did you figure out that it is important to know your audience before you start writing?

Ask students to qualify or restrict some of their conclusions:

- If you wrote a piece for one audience and then found out a different audience needed to read it, could you rewrite it for the other audience?

Ask students to examine their elaborations from different perspectives:

- Who might have a different perspective?

- How might you write for an uninformed audience that is neither hostile nor sympathetic?

Grade 7 Mathematics

Consider the following mathematics standard.

> 7.SP.B.4: Use measures of center and measures of variability for numerical data from random samples to draw informal comparative inferences about two populations. (NGA & CCSSO, 2010c, p. 50)

A teacher using this standard in a questioning sequence could focus on the following:

- Students will understand what different measures of center and measures of variability are.

- Students will be able to calculate different measures of center and measures of variability.

- Students will understand what populations are.

- Students will understand what a random sample is.

- Students will understand what comparative inferences are and will be able to draw comparative inferences from data.

- Students will be able to make inferences based on measures of center and variability.

In this example, we focus on understanding what different measures of center and measures of variability are.

Details

To begin the questioning sequence, the teacher asks students about **human constructs** such as mean, median, mode, range, interquartile range, variance, and standard deviation.

- What is each of the following? (*concept*)

  - Mean
  - Median
  - Mode
  - Range
  - Interquartile range
  - Variance
  - Standard deviation

- What does each of the following measure? (*measurement, quantity, or quality*)

  - Mean
  - Median
  - Mode
  - Range
  - Interquartile range
  - Variance
  - Standard deviation

- How does each of the following help someone make sense of data? (*organize the world*)

  - Mean
  - Median

- Mode
- Range
- Interquartile range
- Variance
- Standard deviation

Category

Teachers should select a category or categories based on their focus for a unit. In this example, the teacher focuses questions on two categories: measures of center and measures of variability.

Ask students to identify examples within a category:

- What are examples of measures of center? Measures of variability?

Ask students to describe the general characteristics of a category:

- What do all measures of center have in common? Measures of variability?

- What are measures of center used for? Measures of variability? (*purpose*)

- What do measures of center measure? Measures of variability? (*causes or consequences*)

Ask students to make comparisons within and across categories:

- Compare the mean to the median. (within-category comparison—measures of center)

- Compare the mean to the standard deviation. (across-category comparison—measure of center to measure of variability)

Elaboration

Elaboration questions build on students' answers to category questions. Therefore, the teacher uses students' responses to category questions to construct elaboration questions.

Ask students to explain reasons for characteristics (Why? questions):

- Why do measures of center show what most of the data look like?

- Why do measures of variability show how spread out the data are?

Ask students to describe the effects of specific characteristics:

- What effect do measures of variability have on measures of center?

- What effect do outliers have on the mean?

Ask students to project what might occur under certain conditions (What if? questions):

- What if you eliminate outliers from a data set?

- What if you include an extreme outlier when calculating a mean?

Evidence

If students conclude that measures of variability show how reliable measures of center are, the teacher can prompt students to provide evidence for their conclusions.

Ask students to identify sources that support their elaborations:

- What sources support your claim?

Ask students to explain the reasoning they used to construct their elaborations:

- How did you figure out that measures of variability show the reliability of measures of center?

Ask students to qualify or restrict some of their conclusions:

- Is there ever a time when measures of variability don't show the reliability of measures of center?

Ask students to examine their elaborations from different perspectives:

- Why might someone only give a measure of center, but not a measure of variability, for a data set?

Grade 8 Reading

Consider the following English language arts standard.

> RI.8.4: Determine the meaning of words and phrases as they are used in a text, including figurative, connotative, and technical meanings; analyze the impact of specific word choices on meaning and tone, including analogies or allusions to other texts. (NGA & CCSSO, 2010a, p. 39)

A teacher using this standard in a questioning sequence could focus on the following:

- Students will understand what figurative, connotative, and technical meanings are.

- Students will be able to determine the meaning of a word or phrase.

- Students will be able to identify specific word choices made by an author.

- Students will be able to analyze the impact of specific word choices.

- Students will understand what tone is.

- Students will understand what an analogy is.

- Students will understand what an allusion is.

- Students will be able to analyze analogies and allusions.

In this example, we focus on understanding what figurative, connotative, and technical meanings are.

Details

To begin the questioning sequence, the teacher asks students about **human constructs** that can have figurative, connotative, or technical meanings.

- What is each of the following? (*concept*)

    - Personification

    - Hyperbole

    - Metaphor

    - Alliteration

    - Simile

- Onomatopoeia

- Idiom

- Allusion

- Definition

- Why do authors use each of the following? (*measurement, quantity, or quality*)

  - Personification

  - Hyperbole

  - Metaphor

  - Alliteration

  - Simile

  - Onomatopoeia

  - Idiom

  - Allusion

  - Definition

- What is a connotative meaning? (*concept*)

- How does figurative language help organize the world? (*organize the world*)

- How do definitions help organize the world? (*organize the world*)

Category

Teachers should select a category or categories based on their focus for a unit. In this example, the teacher focuses questions on three categories: figurative language, connotative language, and technical language.

Ask students to identify examples within a category:

- What are examples of figurative language? Connotative language? Technical language?

Ask students to describe the general characteristics of a category:

- What do all the examples of figurative language have in common? Connotative language? Technical language?

- Why do authors use figurative language? Connotative language? Technical language? (*purpose*)

- How does figurative language affect a text's message? Connotative language? Technical language? (*causes or consequences*)

Ask students to make comparisons within and across categories:

- Compare alliteration to onomatopoeia. (within-category comparison—figurative language)

- Compare an idiom to a definition. (across-category comparison—connotative language to technical language)

Elaboration

Elaboration questions build on students' answers to category questions. Therefore, the teacher uses students' responses to category questions to construct elaboration questions.

Ask students to explain reasons for characteristics (Why? questions):

- Why are figurative and connotative language typically not used in technical writing?

- Why does figurative language make writing more expressive?

- Why can connotative language add ideas to writing?

Ask students to describe the effects of specific characteristics:

- What effect does technical language have on a text? Figurative language? Connotative language?

Ask students to project what might occur under certain conditions (What if? questions):

- What if you replace definitions with figurative or connotative language in a set of technical directions?

Evidence

If students conclude that figurative language makes writing more expressive by reminding readers of real life, the teacher can prompt students to provide evidence for their conclusions.

Ask students to identify sources that support their elaborations:

- What sources can you cite for your conclusion?

Ask students to explain the reasoning they used to construct their elaborations:

- How did you figure out that figurative language reminds readers of real life?

Ask students to qualify or restrict some of their conclusions:

- Are there times when figurative language doesn't remind readers of real life?

Ask students to examine their elaborations from different perspectives:

- What would you say to someone who said that figurative and connotative language are the same?

High School Writing

Consider the following English language arts standards.

> W.11–12.1: Write arguments to support claims in an analysis of substantive topics or texts, using valid reasoning and relevant and sufficient evidence.
>
> a. Introduce precise, knowledgeable claim(s), establish the significance of the claim(s), distinguish the claim(s) from alternate or opposing claims, and create an organization that logically sequences claim(s), counterclaims, reasons, and evidence.
>
> b. Develop claim(s) and counterclaims fairly and thoroughly, supplying the most relevant evidence for each while pointing out the strengths and limitations of both in a manner that anticipates the audience's knowledge level, concerns, values, and possible biases.

c. Use words, phrases, and clauses as well as varied syntax to link the major sections of the text, create cohesion, and clarify the relationships between claim(s) and reasons, between reasons and evidence, and between claim(s) and counterclaims.

d. Establish and maintain a formal style and objective tone while attending to the norms and conventions of the discipline in which they are writing.

e. Provide a concluding statement or section that follows from and supports the argument presented. (NGA & CCSSO, 2010a, p. 45)

A teacher using this standard in a questioning sequence could focus on the following:

- Students will understand what the structure of an argument looks like and will be able to use an argument structure to support claims.

- Students will be able to introduce a claim.

- Students will be able to develop a claim.

- Students will be able to identify major sections of a text they have written.

- Students will be able to identify and clarify relationships between claims and evidence.

- Students will understand what formal style looks and sounds like and will be able to establish and maintain a formal style.

In this example, we focus on understanding what formal style and objective tone look and sound like.

Details

To begin the questioning sequence, the teacher asks students about the **human constructs** of formal style and objective tone.

- What does a formal style sound like? An objective tone? (*concept*)

- Why is formal style important when writing arguments? An objective tone? (*measurement, quantity, or quality*)

Category

Teachers should select a category or categories based on their focus for a unit. In this example, the teacher focuses questions on two categories: texts that use a formal style and texts that use an objective tone.

Ask students to identify examples within a category:

- What are examples of texts that use a formal style? Texts that use an objective tone?

Ask students to describe the general characteristics of a category:

- What are the characteristics of texts that use a formal style? Texts that use an objective tone?

- What purpose or use is associated with texts that use a formal style? Texts that use an objective tone? (*purpose*)

- What causes or consequences are associated with texts that use a formal style? Texts that use an objective tone? (*causes or consequences*)

Ask students to make comparisons within and across categories:

- Compare the style of a research article to the style in a nonfiction book. (within-category comparison—texts that use a formal style)

- Compare the style of a research article to the tone of a biography. (across-category comparison—text that uses a formal style to text that uses an objective tone)

Elaboration

Elaboration questions build on students' answers to category questions. Therefore, the teacher uses students' responses to category questions to construct elaboration questions.

Ask students to explain reasons for characteristics (Why? questions):

- Why does a formal style make it easier for a wider audience to understand a text?

- Why does an objective tone add credibility to a text?

- Why does using a formal style usually mean writing in third person?

- Why does an objective tone avoid misunderstandings?

Ask students to describe the effects of specific characteristics:

- What effect does using correct punctuation and spelling have on an author's credibility?

- What effect does sounding authoritative have on an author's credibility?

Ask students to project what might occur under certain conditions (What if? questions):

- What if a research article was written in first or second person, using slang?

Evidence

If students concluded that a formal style and objective tone gives an author credibility because it shows he or she is considerate of the reader (he or she makes it easier for the reader to understand and follow what is written), the teacher can prompt students to provide evidence for their conclusions.

Ask students to identify sources that support their elaborations:

- What sources support your claim?

Ask students to explain the reasoning they used to construct their elaborations:

- Explain the reasoning behind your conclusion.

Ask students to qualify or restrict some of their conclusions:

- Is it possible for writers who don't use a formal style and objective tone to establish credibility?

Ask students to find errors in the reasoning used to construct their elaborations:

- What error is being committed when writers are overly familiar with their readers?

Ask students to examine their elaborations from different perspectives:

- When might an author writing an argument not want to use a formal style?

High School Mathematics

Consider the following mathematics standards.

> HSF-IF.C.7: Graph functions expressed symbolically and show key features of the graph, by hand in simple cases and using technology for more complicated cases.
>
> a. Graph linear and quadratic functions and show intercepts, maxima, and minima.
>
> b. Graph square root, cube root, and piecewise-defined functions, including step functions and absolute value functions.
>
> c. Graph polynomial functions, identifying zeros when suitable factorizations are available, and showing end behavior.
>
> d. Graph rational functions, identifying zeros and asymptotes when suitable factorizations are available, and showing end behavior.
>
> e. Graph exponential and logarithmic functions, showing intercepts and end behavior, and trigonometric functions, showing period, midline, and amplitude. (NGA & CCSSO, 2010c, p. 69)

A teacher using this standard in a questioning sequence could focus on the following:

- Students will be able to graph functions.

- Students will understand what intercepts, maxima, and minima are and will be able to show them when graphing functions.

- Students will understand what zeros and asymptotes are and will be able to identify them when suitable factorizations are available.

- Students will understand what end behavior is and will be able to show end behavior when graphing functions.

- Students will understand what period, midline, and amplitude are and will be able to show them when graphing functions.

In this example, we focus on understanding the characteristics of different types of functions.

Details

To begin the questioning sequence, the teacher asks students about specific kinds of functions. Here, we consider types of functions to be **human constructs**.

- What kind of relationship does each of the following functions express? (*measurement, quantity, or quality*)

  - Linear function
  - Quadratic function
  - Square root function
  - Cube root function
  - Piecewise-defined function
  - Step function
  - Absolute value function
  - Polynomial function

- Rational function
- Exponential function
- Logarithmic function
- What does the graph of each of the following functions look like? (*concept*)
  - Linear function
  - Quadratic function
  - Square root function
  - Cube root function
  - Piecewise-defined function
  - Step function
  - Absolute value function
  - Polynomial function
  - Rational function
  - Exponential function
  - Logarithmic function

Category

Teachers should select a category or categories based on their focus for a unit. In this example, the teacher focuses questions on three categories: polynomial functions, root functions, and piecewise functions.

Ask students to identify examples within a category:

- What are examples of polynomial functions? Root functions? Piecewise functions?

Ask students to describe the general characteristics of a category:

- What are the characteristics of polynomial functions? Root functions? Piecewise functions?
- What are polynomial functions used for? Root functions? Piecewise functions? (*purpose*)
- What causes or consequences are associated with polynomial functions? Root functions? Piecewise functions? (*causes or consequences*)

Ask students to make comparisons within and across categories:

- Compare a linear function to a quadratic function. (within-category comparison—polynomial functions)
- Compare a linear function to an absolute value function. (across-category comparison—polynomial function to piecewise function)

Elaboration

Elaboration questions build on students' answers to category questions. Therefore, the teacher uses students' responses to category questions to construct elaboration questions.

Ask students to explain reasons for characteristics (Why? questions):

- Why do polynomial functions model many real-life situations?

- Why can polynomial functions be used to analyze costs?

Ask students to describe the effects of specific characteristics:

- What effect does the domain of a function have on its range?

- What effect do exponents, roots, or absolute values have on functions?

Ask students to project what might occur under certain conditions (What if? questions):

- What if a value in the domain of a function were related to more than one value in the range?

- What if a vertical line crossed the same value more than once in the graph of a function?

Evidence

If students conclude that any relationship in which a value in the domain is related to more than one value in the range is not a function, the teacher can prompt students to provide evidence for their conclusions.

Ask students to identify sources that support their elaborations:

- What sources do you have to support your claim?

Ask students to explain the reasoning they used to construct their elaborations:

- How did you figure out your conclusion?

Ask students to qualify or restrict some of their conclusions:

- Is there ever a time when a value in the domain might be related to more than one value in the range of a function?

High School Science

Consider the following science standard.

> HS-PS3-4: Plan and conduct an investigation to provide evidence that the transfer of thermal energy when two components of different temperature are combined within a closed system results in a more uniform energy distribution among the components in the system (second law of thermodynamics). (Achieve, 2013, p. 86)

A teacher using this standard in a questioning sequence could focus on the following:

- Students will be able to plan an investigation.

- Students will be able to conduct an investigation.

- Students will be able to provide evidence.

- Students will understand the second law of thermodynamics and will be able to recognize examples of it.

- Students will be able to explain with numbers (quantitatively) what is happening when energy is distributed between two components.

- Students will be able to explain with words (conceptually) what is happening when energy is distributed between two components.

In this example, we focus on understanding the second law of thermodynamics and recognizing examples of it.

Details

To begin the questioning sequence, the teacher asks students about the **natural phenomenon** of energy distribution.

- Where does energy distribution occur? (*places*)

- How long does energy distribution take? (*time*)

- What happens during energy distribution? (*happened/happens*)

Category

Teachers should select a category or categories based on their focus for a unit. In this example, the teacher focuses questions on two categories: processes that distribute energy and processes that concentrate energy.

Ask students to identify examples within a category:

- What are examples of processes that distribute energy? Processes that concentrate energy?

Ask students to describe the general characteristics of a category:

- What are characteristics of processes that distribute energy? Processes that concentrate energy?

- What sequence of events occurs when energy is distributed? When energy is concentrated? (*process*)

- What causes and consequences are associated with processes that distribute energy? Processes that concentrate energy? (*causes and consequences*)

- What places are associated with processes that distribute energy? Processes that concentrate energy? (*places*)

Ask students to make comparisons within and across categories:

- Compare putting ice in boiling water to eating ice cream. (within-category comparison—processes that distribute energy)

- Compare putting ice in boiling water to freezing water to make ice. (across-category comparison—process that distributes energy to process that concentrates energy)

Elaboration

Elaboration questions build on students' answers to category questions. Therefore, the teacher uses students' responses to category questions to construct elaboration questions.

Ask students to explain reasons for characteristics (Why? questions):

- Why does energy spread out when two components of different temperatures meet?

- Why is energy less useful after it is distributed?

Ask students to describe the effects of specific characteristics:

- What effect does energy have on temperature?

- What effect does temperature have on energy distribution?

Ask students to project what might occur under certain conditions (What if? questions):

- What if energy is not added to a system?

Evidence

If students conclude that energy becomes less useful over time unless additional "fresh" energy is used to concentrate it into useful forms, the teacher can prompt students to provide evidence for their conclusions.

Ask students to identify sources that support their elaborations:

- What sources support your claim?

Ask students to explain the reasoning they used to construct their elaborations:

- How did you figure out that energy becomes less useful over time unless additional "fresh" energy is added?

Ask students to qualify or restrict some of their conclusions:

- Where does "fresh" energy come from?

Ask students to find errors in the reasoning used to construct their elaborations:

- What errors might a listener make if he or she only heard your claim?

Ask students to examine their elaborations from different perspectives:

- How might things function differently in space or on another planet?

REFERENCES AND RESOURCES

Aagard, S. A. (1973). Oral questioning by the teacher: Influence on student achievement in eleventh grade chemistry (Doctoral dissertation, New York University). *Dissertation Abstracts International, 34,* 631A.

Achieve. (2013). *Next Generation Science Standards: DCI arrangements of the Next Generation Science Standards.* Washington, DC: Author. Accessed at http://63960de18916c597c345-8e3bed018c b857642bed25a591e65353.r63.cf1.rackcdn.com/K-12%20DCIs%20Combined%206.11.13.pdf on October 17, 2013.

Adams, T. H. (1964). *The development of a method for analysis of questions asked by teachers in classroom discussion* (Doctoral dissertation). University Microfilms. (64–2809)

Anderson, L. W., & Krathwohl, D. R. (Eds.). (2001). *A taxonomy for learning, teaching, and assessing: A revision of Bloom's Taxonomy of Educational Objectives* (Abridged ed.). New York: Longman.

Aschner, M. J. (1961). Asking questions to trigger thinking. *NEA Journal, 51,* 44–46.

AT&T. (2013). *Samsung Galaxy S4 Active: Whatever-proof* [Video file]. Accessed at www.ispot.tv /ad/7tAC/at-and-t-samsung-galaxy-s4-active-whatever-proof on July 31, 2013.

Bălescu, A., Nemet, C., Zamfir, C., Ispas, D., & Idomir, M. (2013). Identifying risk factors for symptoms of severe trichinellosis: A case study of 143 infected persons in Brasov, Romania 2001–2008. *Vet Parasitol, 194,* 142–144.

Beatty, I. D., & Gerace, W. J. (2009). Technology-enhanced formative assessment: A research-based pedagogy for teaching science with classroom response technology. *Journal of Science Education and Technology, 18,* 146–162.

Beck, I. L., McKeown, M. G., Hamilton, R. L., & Kucan, L. (1997). *Questioning the author: An approach for enhancing student engagement with text.* Delaware: International Reading Association.

Bedwell, L. E. (1974). The effects of training teachers in question-asking skills on the achievement and attitudes of elementary pupils (Doctoral dissertation, Indiana University). *Dissertation Abstracts International, 35,* 5980–09A.

Beseda, C. G. (1973). Levels of questioning used by student teachers and its effects on pupil achievement and critical thinking ability (Doctoral dissertation, North Texas State University). *Dissertation Abstracts International, 32,* 2543A.

Bloom, B. S. (Ed.). (1956). *Taxonomy of educational objectives: The classification of educational goals. Handbook 1: Cognitive domain*. New York: Longmans, Green.

Brophy, J. (1973). Stability of teacher effectiveness. *American Educational Research Journal, 10*, 245–252.

Brophy, J., & Evertson, C. (1974a). *Process-product correlations in the Texas Teacher Effectiveness Study: Final report* (Research Report No. 74–4). Austin: University of Texas, R & D Center for Teacher Education.

Brophy, J., & Evertson, C. (1974b). *The Texas Teacher Effectiveness Project: Presentation of non-linear relationships and summary discussion* (Research Report No. 74–6). Austin: University of Texas, R & D Center for Teacher Education.

Brophy, J. E., & Evertson, C. M. (1976). *Learning from teaching: A developmental perspective*. Boston: Allyn & Bacon.

Brophy, J., & Good, T. L. (1986). Teacher behavior and student achievement. In M. C. Wittrock (Ed.), *Handbook of research on teaching* (3rd ed.; pp. 328–373). New York: Macmillan.

Brown, G. A., & Edmondson, R. (1984). Asking questions. In E. C. Wragg (Ed.), *Classroom teaching skills* (pp. 97–120). London: Routledge.

Bruff, D. (2009). *Teaching with classroom response systems: Creating active learning environments*. San Francisco: Jossey-Bass.

Buggey, L. J. (1971). A study of the relationship of classroom questions and social studies achievement of second-grade children (Doctoral dissertation, University of Washington). *Dissertation Abstracts International, 32*, 2543A.

Burbules, N. C., & Callister, T. A., Jr. (2000). *Watch IT: The risks and promises of information technologies for education*. Boulder, CO: Westview Press.

Carner, R. L. (1963). Levels of questioning. *Education, 83*, 546–550.

Clark, C. M., Gage, N. L., Marx, R. W., Peterson, P. L., Stayrook, N. G., & Winne, P. H. (1979). A factorial experiment on teacher structuring, soliciting, and reacting. *Journal of Educational Psychology, 71*(4), 534–552.

Clements, R. D. (1964). Art student-teacher questioning. *Studies in Art Education, 6*(1), 14–19.

Coiro, J. (2005). Making sense of online text. *Educational Leadership, 63*(2), 30–35.

Craig, S. D., Sullins, J., Witherspoon, A., & Gholson, B. (2006). The deep-level-reasoning-question effect: The role of dialogue and deep-level-reasoning questions during vicarious learning. *Cognition and Instruction, 24*(4), 565–591.

Dahllöf, U. S., & Lundgren, U. P. (1970). *Project Compass 23: Macro and micro approaches combined for curriculum process analysis: A Swedish educational field project*. Paper presented at the annual meeting of the American Educational Research Association, Minneapolis.

Dantonio, M., & Beisenherz, P. C. (2001). *Learning to question, questioning to learn: Developing effective teacher questioning practices*. Boston: Allyn & Bacon.

David, J. L. (2009). What research says about . . . Teaching media literacy. *Educational Leadership, 66*(6), 84–86.

Davide Pedersoli & C. (2010a). *Brown Bess.* Accessed at www.davide-pedersoli.com/scheda-prodotto .asp/l_en/idpr_67/rifles-brown-bess-brown-bess.html on October 23, 2013.

Davide Pedersoli & C. (2010b). *1763 leger (1766) Charleville.* Accessed at www.davide-pedersoli.com /tipologia-prodotti.asp/l_en/idt_46/rifles-1763-leger-1766-charleville.html on October 23, 2013.

Davide Pedersoli & C. (2010c). *Kentucky flintlock model.* Accessed at www.davide-pedersoli.com/scheda -prodotto.asp/l_en/idpr_91/rifles-kentucky-kentucky-flintlock-model.html on October 23, 2013.

Driscoll, D. M., Craig, S. D., Gholson, B., Ventura, M., & Graesser, A. C. (2003). Vicarious learning: Effects of overhearing dialog and monologue-like discourse in a virtual tutoring session. *Journal of Educational Computing Research, 29,* 431–450.

Dunkin, M. (1978). Student characteristics, classroom processes, and student achievement. *Journal of Educational Psychology, 70,* 998–1009.

Dunkin, M. J., & Biddle, B. J. (1974). *The study of teaching.* New York: Holt, Rinehart, and Winston.

Dupouy-Camet, J. (2000). Trichinellosis: A worldwide zoonosis. *Vet Parasitol, 93*(3–4), 191–200.

Engineer comp geek. (2009). *File:Musketparts.jpg.* Accessed at http://en.wikipedia.org/wiki/File :Musketparts.jpg on September 13, 2013.

Evertson, C., & Brophy, J. (1973). High-inference behavioral ratings as correlates of teaching effective-ness. *JSAS Catalog of Selected Documents in Psychology, 3,* 97.

Evertson, C., & Brophy, J. (1974). *Texas Teacher Effectiveness Project: Questionnaire and interview data* (Research Report No. 74–5). Austin: University of Texas, R & D Center for Teacher Education.

Floyd, W. D. (1960). *An analysis of the oral questioning activity in selected Colorado primary classrooms* (Doctoral dissertation). University Microfilms. (60–6253)

Furst, N. F. (1967). The effects of training in interaction analysis on the behavior of student teachers in secondary schools. In E. J. Amidon & J. B. Hough (Eds.), *Interaction analysis: Theory, research and application* (pp. 315–327). Reading, MA: Addison-Wesley.

Furst, N. F., & Amidon, E. J. (1967). Teacher-pupil interaction patterns in the elementary school. In E. J. Amidon & J. B. Hough (Eds.), *Interaction analysis: Theory, research and application* (pp. 167–175). Reading, MA: Addison-Wesley.

Gage, N. L., & Berliner, D. C. (1984). *Educational psychology* (3rd ed.). Boston: Houghton Mifflin.

Gage, N. L., & Stanford Program on Teaching Effectiveness. (1976). A factorially designed experiment on teacher structuring, soliciting, and reacting. *Journal of Teacher Education, 27*(1), 35–38.

Gall, M. D. (1970). The use of questions in teaching. *Review of Educational Research, 40*(5), 707–721.

Gall, M. D. (1975). *The effects of teacher use of questioning techniques on student achievement and attitudes, vol. I* (Final report). San Francisco: Far West Laboratory for Educational Research and Development.

Gall, M. (1984). Synthesis of research on teachers' questioning. *Educational Leadership, 42*(3), 40–47.

Gall, M. D., & Rhody, T. (1987). Review of research on questioning techniques. In W. W. Wilen (Ed.), *Questions, questioning techniques, and effective teaching* (pp. 23–48). Washington, DC: NEA Professional Library, National Education Association.

Gall, M. D., Ward, B. A., Berliner, D. C., Cahen, L. S., Winne, P. H., Elashoff, J. D., et al. (1978). Effects of questioning techniques and recitation on student learning. *American Educational Research Journal, 15*(2), 175–199.

Gallagher, J. J. (1965). Expressive thought by gifted children in the classroom. *Elementary English, 42*(5), 559–568.

Gambrell, L. B. (1983). The occurrence of think-time during reading comprehension instruction. *Journal of Educational Research, 77*(2), 77–80.

Gandel, S. (2013, April 17). *Damn Excel! How the 'most important software application of all time' is ruining the world.* Accessed at http://finance.fortune.cnn.com/2013/04/17/rogoff-reinhart-excel -errors/ on August 6, 2013.

Garmston, R. J., & Wellman, B. M. (2009). *The adaptive school: A sourcebook for developing collaborative groups* (2nd ed.). Norwood, MA: Christopher-Gordon.

Gayle, B. M., Preiss, R. W., & Allen, M. (2006). How effective are teacher-initiated classroom questions in enhancing student learning? In B. M. Gayle, R. W. Preiss, N. Burrell, & M. Allen (Eds.), *Classroom communication and instructional processes: Advances through meta-analysis* (pp. 279– 293). Mahwah, NJ: Erlbaum.

Ghee, H. J. (1975). A study of the effects of high level cognitive questions on the levels of response and critical thinking abilities in students of two social problems classes (Doctoral dissertation, University of Virginia). *Dissertation Abstracts International, 36,* 5187–08A.

Gholson, B., & Craig, S. D. (2006). Promoting constructive activities that support vicarious learning during computer-based instruction. *Educational Psychology Review, 18,* 119–139.

Good, T. L., & Brophy, J. E. (2003). *Looking in classrooms* (9th ed.). Boston: Allyn & Bacon.

Graesser, A. C., & McMahen, C. L. (1993). Anomalous information triggers questions when adults solve quantitative problems and comprehend stories. *Journal of Educational Psychology, 85*(1), 136–151.

Graesser, A. C., & Olde, B. A. (2003). How does one know whether a person understands a device? The quality of the questions the person asks when the device breaks down. *Journal of Educational Psychology, 95*(3), 524–536.

Guilford, J. P. (1959). Three faces of intellect. *American Psychologist, 14*(8), 469–479.

Guszak, F. J. (1967). Teacher questioning and reading. *The Reading Teacher, 21*(3), 227–234.

Hannel, I. (2009). Insufficient questioning. *Kappan, 91*(3), 65–69.

Hare, V. C., & Pulliam, C. A. (1980). Teacher questioning: A verification and an extension. *Journal of Literacy Research, 12*(1), 69–72.

Hattie, J. (2009). *Visible learning: A synthesis of over 800 meta-analyses relating to achievement.* New York: Routledge.

Hill, W. E. (1915). My wife and my mother-in-law. *Puck, 78*(2018), 11. Accessed at http://en.wikipedia .org/wiki/File:My_Wife_and_My_Mother-in-Law.jpg on November 1, 2013.

Hunkins, F. P. (1968). The influence of analysis and evaluation questions on achievement in sixth grade social studies. *Educational Leadership Research Supplement, 1,* 326–332.

Johnson, D. W., & Johnson, R. T. (2005). *Teaching students to be peacemakers* (4th ed.). Edina, MN: Interaction Book.

Kagan, S., & Kagan, M. (2009). *Kagan cooperative learning.* San Clemente, CA: Kagan.

Kendall, J. S., & Marzano, R. J. (2000). *Content knowledge: A compendium of standards and benchmarks for K–12 education* (3rd ed.). Alexandria, VA: Association for Supervision and Curriculum Development.

King, A. (1992). Comparison of self-questioning, summarizing, and notetaking-review as strategies for learning from lectures. *American Educational Research Journal, 29*(2), 303–323.

King, A. (1994). Guiding knowledge construction in the classroom: Effects of teaching children how to question and how to explain. *American Educational Research Journal, 31*(2), 303–323.

Kintsch, W. (1988). The role of knowledge in discourse comprehension: A construction-integration model. *Psychological Review, 95*(2), 163–182.

Kirsch, I. S., & Mosenthal, P. B. (1989). Building documents by combining simple lists. *Journal of Reading, 33*(2), 132–135.

Kirsch, I. S., & Mosenthal, P. B. (1990a). Mimetic documents: Diagrams. *Journal of Reading, 34*(4), 290–294.

Kirsch, I. S., & Mosenthal, P. B. (1990b). Mimetic documents: Pictures. *Journal of Reading, 34*(3), 216–220.

Kirsch, I. S., & Mosenthal, P. B. (1990c). Nested lists. *Journal of Reading, 33*(4), 294–297.

Kirsch, I. S., & Mosenthal, P. B. (1991). Understanding mimetic documents through "knowledge modeling." *Journal of Reading, 34*(7), 552–558.

Kirsch, I. S., & Mosenthal, P. B. (1992). How to navigate a document using locate known/need-to-know strategies. *Journal of Reading, 36*(2), 140–144.

Kleinman, G. S. (1965). Teachers' questions and student understanding of science. *Journal of Research in Science Teaching, 3*(4), 307–317.

Kuiper, E., Volman, M., & Terwel, J. (2005). The web as an information resource in K–12 education: Strategies for supporting students in searching and processing information. *Review of Educational Research, 75*(3), 285–328.

Ladd, G. T., & Anderson, H. O. (1970). Determining the level of inquiry in teachers' questions. *Journal of Research in Science Teaching, 7*(4), 395–400.

Levin, T. (with Long, R.). (1981). *Effective instruction.* Alexandria, VA: Association for Supervision and Curriculum Development.

Lucking, R. A. (1975). A study of the effects of a hierarchically-ordered questioning technique on adolescents' responses to short stories (Doctoral dissertation, University of Nebraska). *Dissertation Abstracts International, 36*, 0138–08A.

Martikean, A. (1973). *The levels of questioning and their effects upon student performance above the knowledge level of Bloom's taxonomy of educational objectives* (Research Paper No. E585, Division of Education). Gary: Indiana University Northwest.

Marzano, R. J. (with Marzano, J. S., & Pickering, D. J.). (2003). *Classroom management that works: Research-based strategies for every teacher.* Alexandria, VA: Association for Supervision and Curriculum Development.

Marzano, R. J. (2007). *The art and science of teaching: A comprehensive framework for effective instruction.* Alexandria, VA: Association for Supervision and Curriculum Development.

Marzano, R. J., Frontier, T., & Livingston, D. (2011). *Effective supervision: Supporting the art and science of teaching.* Alexandria, VA: Association for Supervision and Curriculum Development.

Marzano, R. J., Pickering, D. J., & Pollock, J. E. (2001). *Classroom instruction that works: Research-based strategies for increasing student achievement.* Alexandria, VA: Association for Supervision and Curriculum Development.

Mathes, C. A. (1977). The effects of two different reading comprehension achievement of students at a fourth grade reading level. (Doctoral dissertation, Indiana University Nebraska). *Dissertation Abstracts International, 39,* 7139–40A.

Mazur, E. (1997). *Peer instruction: A user's manual.* Upper Saddle River, NJ: Prentice Hall.

Meyer, B. J. F. (1982). Reading research and the composition teacher: The importance of plans. *College Composition and Communication, 33*(1), 37–49.

Meyer, B. J. F., Young, C. J., & Bartlett, B. J. (1989). *Memory improved: Reading and memory enhancement across the life span through strategic text structures.* Hillsdale, NJ: Erlbaum.

Millett, G. B. (1968). Comparison of four teacher training procedures in achieving teacher and pupil "translation" behaviors in secondary school social studies (Doctoral dissertation, Stanford University). *Dissertation Abstracts International, 28,* 4514A.

Mosenthal, P., & Kirsch, I. (1989a). Lists: The building blocks of documents. *Journal of Reading, 33*(1), 58–60.

Mosenthal, P. B., & Kirsch, I. S. (1989b). Intersecting lists. *Journal of Reading, 33*(3), 210–213.

Mosenthal, P. B., & Kirsch, I. S. (1990a). Understanding general reference maps. *Journal of Reading, 34*(1), 60–63.

Mosenthal, P. B., & Kirsch, I. S. (1990b). Understanding graphs and charts, part I. *Journal of Reading, 33*(5), 371–373.

Mosenthal, P. B., & Kirsch, I. S. (1990c). Understanding graphs and charts, part II. *Journal of Reading, 33*(6), 454–457.

Mosenthal, P. B., & Kirsch, I. S. (1990d). Understanding thematic maps. *Journal of Reading, 34*(2), 136–140.

Mosenthal, P. B., & Kirsch, I. S. (1991a). Information types in nonmimetic documents: A review of Biddle's wipe-clean slate. *Journal of Reading, 34*(8), 654–660.

Mosenthal, P. B., & Kirsch, I. S. (1991b). Mimetic documents: Process schematics. *Journal of Reading, 34*(5), 390–397.

Mosenthal, P. B., & Kirsch, I. S. (1991c). More mimetic documents: Procedural schematics. *Journal of Reading, 34*(6), 486–490.

Mosenthal, P. B., & Kirsch, I. S. (1992). Cycle strategies in document search: From here to there to wherever. *Journal of Reading, 36*(3), 238–242.

Moyer, J. R. (1966). *An exploratory study of questioning in the instructional processes in selected elementary schools* (Doctoral dissertation). University Microfilms. (66–2661)

Nash, R. J., & Shiman, D. A. (1974). The English teacher as questioner. *English Journal, 63*, 42–45.

National Governors Association Center for Best Practices & Council of Chief State School Officers. (2010a). *Common Core State Standards for English language arts and literacy in history/social science, science, & technical subjects.* Washington, DC: Authors.

National Governors Association Center for Best Practices & Council of Chief State School Officers. (2010b). *Common Core State Standards for English language arts & literacy in history/social studies, science, and technical subjects—Appendix A: Research supporting key elements of the standards and glossary of key terms.* Washington, DC: Authors.

National Governors Association Center for Best Practices & Council of Chief State School Officers. (2010c). *Common Core State Standards for mathematics.* Washington, DC: Authors.

Otero, J., & Graesser, A. C. (2001). PREG: Elements of a model of question asking. *Cognition and Instruction, 19*(2), 143–175.

Pashler, H., Bain, P. M., Bottge, B. A., Graesser, A., Doedinger, K., McDaniel, M., & Metcalfe, J. (2007). *Organizing instruction and study to improve student learning* [NCER 2007–2004]. Washington, DC: National Center for Education Research, Institute of Education Sciences, U.S. Department of Education. Accessed at http://ies.ed.gov/ncee/wwc/pdf/practiceguides/20072004.pdf on January 19, 2011.

Pate, R. T., & Bremer, N. H. (1967). Guiding learning through skillful questioning. *Elementary School Journal, 67*(8), 417–422.

Rankin, B. (2005). *Radical cartography.* Accessed at www.radicalcartography.net/index.html?boston -f-g on September 13, 2013.

Redfield, D. L., & Rousseau, E. W. (1981). A meta-analysis of experimental research on teacher questioning behavior. *Review of Educational Research, 51*(2), 237–245.

Ripley, J. P., II. (1981). The effects of preservice teacher's cognitive questioning level and redirecting on student science achievement. *Journal of Research in Science Teaching, 18*(4), 303–309.

Rogers, V. M. (1968). Varying the cognitive levels of classroom questions in elementary social studies: An analysis of the use of questions by student-teachers (Doctoral dissertation, University of Texas at Austin). *Dissertation Abstracts International, 30*, 1459–04A.

Rosenshine, B. (1971). *Teaching behaviors and student achievement.* Slough, England: National Foundation for Educational Research in England and Wales.

Rosenshine, B. (1976a). Classroom instruction. In N. L. Gage (Ed.), *Psychology of teaching methods: The seventy-fifth yearbook of the National Society for the Study of Education, Part I* (pp. 335–371). Chicago: University of Chicago Press.

Rosenshine, B. (1976b). Recent research on teaching behaviors and student achievement. *Journal of Teacher Education, 27*(1), 61–64.

Rosenshine, B., Meister, C., & Chapman, S. (1996). Teaching students to generate questions: A review of the intervention studies. *Review of Educational Research*, 66(2), 181–221.

Ryan, F. L. (1973). Differentiated effects of levels of questioning on student achievement. *The Journal of Experimental Education*, 41(3), 63–67.

Ryan, F. L. (1974). The effects on social studies achievement of multiple student responding to different levels of questioning. *The Journal of Experimental Education*, 42(4), 71–75.

Samson, G. E., Strykowski, B., Weinstein, T., & Walberg, H. J. (1987). The effects of teacher questioning levels on student achievement: A quantitative synthesis. *Journal of Educational Research*, 80(5), 290–295.

Sanchez, C. A., & Branaghan, R. (2011). Turning to learn: Screen orientation and reasoning with small devices. *Computers in Human Behavior*, 27(2), 793–797.

Sanchez, C. A., & Wiley, J. (2009). To scroll or not to scroll: Scrolling, working memory capacity, and comprehending complex texts. *Human Factors*, 51(5), 730–738.

Sanders, N. M. (1966). *Classroom questions: What kinds?* New York: Harper & Row.

Savage, T. V. (1972). A study of the relationship of classroom questions and social studies achievement of fifth grade children (Doctoral dissertation, University of Washington). *Dissertation Abstracts International*, 33, 2245–05A.

Schreiber, J. E. (1967). *Teachers' question-asking techniques in social studies* (Doctoral dissertation). University Microfilms. (67–9099)

Soar, R. S. (1968). Optimum teacher-pupil interaction for pupil growth. *Educational Leadership*, 26, 275–280.

Soar, R. S. (1973). *Follow Through classroom process measurement and pupil growth* (1970–71, final report). Gainesville: University of Florida, Institute for Development of Human Resources.

Soar, R. S. (1977). An integration of findings from four studies of teacher effectiveness. In G. Borich & K. Fenton (Eds.), *The appraisal of teaching: Concepts and process* (pp. 96–103). Reading, MA: Addison-Wesley.

Soar, R. S., & Soar, R. M. (1972). An empirical analysis of selected Follow Through programs: An example of a process approach to evaluation. In I. Gordon (Ed.), *Early childhood education* (pp. 229–259). Chicago: National Society for the Study of Education.

Soar, R. S., & Soar, R. M. (1973). *Classroom behavior, pupil characteristics and pupil growth for the school year and the summer*. Gainesville: University of Florida, Institute for Development of Human Resources.

Soar, R. S., & Soar, R. M. (1978). *Setting variables, classroom interaction, and multiple pupil outcomes* (Final report, Project No. 6–0432, Grant No. NIE-G-76–0100). Washington, DC: National Institute of Education.

Soar, R. S., & Soar, R. M. (1979). Emotional climate and management. In P. Peterson & H. Walberg (Eds.), *Research on teaching: Concepts, findings and implications* (pp. 97–119). Berkeley, CA: McCutchan.

Spaulding, R. L. (1965). *Achievement, creativity, and self-concept correlates of teacher-pupil transactions in elementary school classrooms*. Hempstead, NY: Hofstra University.

Stallings, J., & Kaskowitz, D. (1974). *Follow Through classroom observation evaluation 1972–1973* (SRI Project URU-7370). Stanford, CA: Stanford Research Institute.

Stallings, J. A., & Kaskowitz, D. H. (1975, April). *A study of Follow Through implementation.* Paper presented at the annual meeting of the American Educational Research Association.

Stevens, R. (1912). *The question as a measure of efficiency in instruction: A critical study of class-room practice.* New York: Teacher's College Press.

Stowell, J. R., & Nelson, J. M. (2007). Benefits of electronic audience response systems on student participation, learning, and emotion. *Teaching of Psychology, 34*(4), 253–258.

U.S. Bureau of the Census. (1975). *Historical statistics of the United States, colonial times to 1970, bicentennial edition, part 1.* Washington, DC: Author.

U.S. Department of Agriculture. (2011). *Parasites and foodborne illness* [Fact sheet]. Accessed at www.fsis.usda.gov/wps/wcm/connect/48a0685a-61ce-4235-b2d7-f07f53a0c7c8/Parasites_and _Foodborne_Illness.pdf?MOD=AJPERES on July 25, 2013.

van Dijk, T. A., & Kintsch, W. (1983). *Strategies of discourse comprehension.* New York: Academic Press.

Ward, B. A., & Tikunoff, W. J. (1975). *Application of research to teaching* (Report A75–2). San Francisco: Far West Laboratory for Educational Research.

Wilen, W. W. (1987). Improving teachers' questions and questioning: Research informs practice. In W. W. Wilen (Ed.), *Questions, questioning techniques, and effective teaching* (pp. 173–200). Washington, DC: NEA Professional Library, National Education Association.

Wilen, W. W., & Clegg, A. A. (1986). Effective questions and questioning: A research review. *Theory and Research in Social Education, 14*(2), 153–161.

Wiley, J., Goldman, S. R., Graesser, A. C., Sanchez, C. A., Ash, I. K., & Hemmerich, J. A. (2009). Source evaluation, comprehension, and learning in Internet science inquiry tasks. *American Educational Research Journal, 46*(4), 1060–1106.

Winne, P. H. (1979). Experiments relating teachers' use of higher cognitive questions to student achievement. *Review of Educational Research, 49*(1), 13–49.

Wisher, R. A., & Graesser, A. C. (2007). Question asking in advanced distributed learning environments. In S. M. Fiore & E. Salas (Eds.), *Toward a science of distributed learning* (pp. 209–234). Washington, DC: American Psychological Association.

Wright, C., & Nuthall, G. (1970). Relationships between teacher behaviors and pupil achievement in three experimental elementary science lessons. *American Educational Research Journal, 7*(4), 477–491.

INDEX

Signature PD Service

Enhancing Reasoning and Argumentation Skills Through Questioning Sequences

Elicit higher-order thinking from students with this on-site workshop. Research indicates that the intentional use of targeted questions in a coordinated sequence is an effective way to prompt the discovery of new information and deepen student learning. Questioning sequences lead students through the process of making an authentic claim and supporting it with evidence.

Discover why individual questions are not a reliable way to encourage students to use higher-order thinking and knowledge application skills. Learn a four-phase process for questioning that prompts students to use the argumentation and reasoning skills highlighted in the college and career readiness anchor standards and mathematical practice standards of the Common Core State Standards.

- Learn the four phases of an effective questioning sequence.

- Understand how students build knowledge and how to scaffold their thinking through appropriate questions about details, categories, elaborations, and evidence.

- Discover research on effective questioning and questioning sequences in the classroom.

- Explore important planning considerations for designing questioning sequences.

- Identify crucial aspects of content to be the target of questioning sequences.

- Align questioning practices in the classroom with the cognitive skills required by the CCSS.

Get started!
marzanoresearch.com/OnsitePD